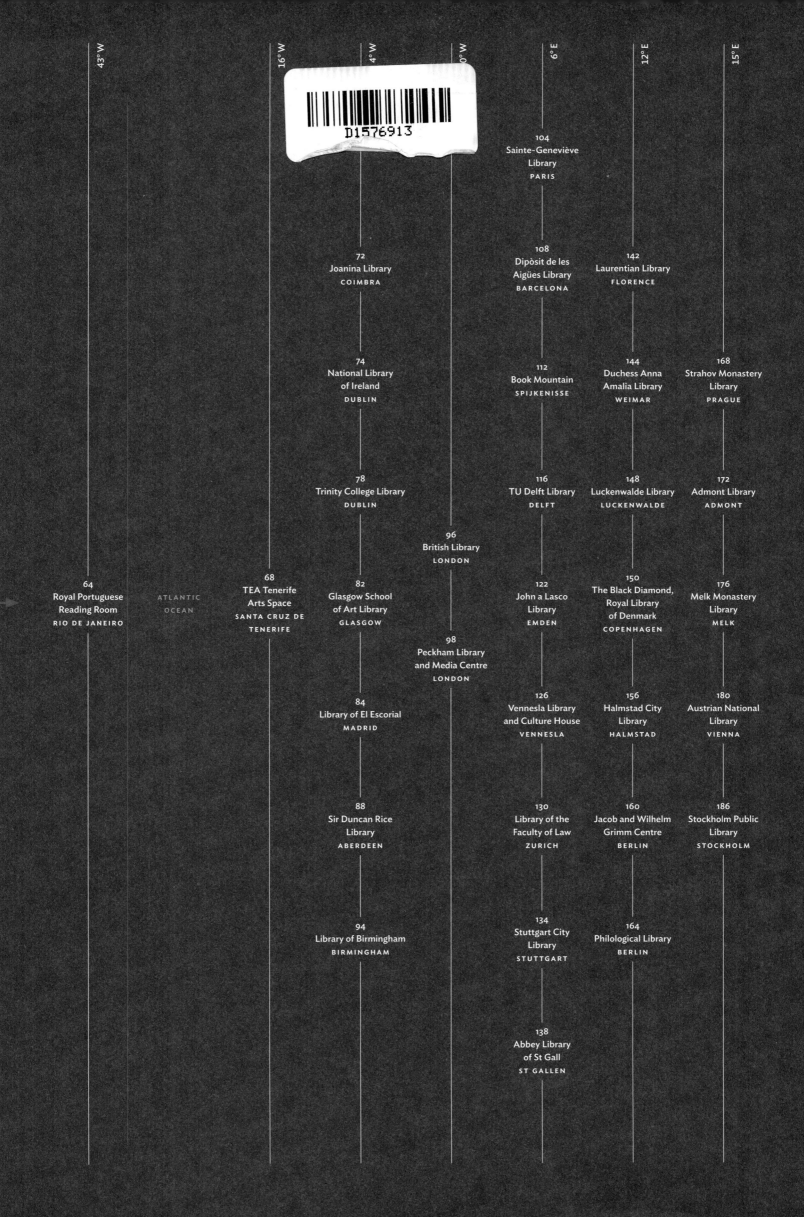

Roads Publishing
19–22 Dame Street
Dublin 2
Ireland

www.roads.co

First published 2014

1

Libraries
Roads Reflections
Text copyright © Roads Publishing
Design and layout copyright © Roads Publishing
Image copyright © the copyright holders; see p. 191
Design by Conor & David

Printed in India

Upper front-cover image:
Long Room, Trinity College Dublin, Mark Colliton
Lower front-cover image:
LiYuan Library, Li Xiaodong Atelier
Back cover image:
Long Room, Trinity College Dublin, Ingram Publishing/
Getty Images

978-1-909399-10-5

LIBRARIES

ROADS

Foreword

Bjarne Hammer
schmidt hammer lassen architects

The library as literary or filmic scenography is iconic. It is often portrayed as a place of mystique and secrecy, as a dim and quiet location, where the protagonist searches for answers and for wisdom. The spectator decodes and recognises the constructed representation of the library as a place to which he or she can relate. It is interesting how the fictional representation of the library often creates a strong sense of atmosphere – a strong sense of place – while it simultaneously differs from the spectator's self-experienced knowledge of the authentic library of today.

Evolution

The library as institution is ancient. Dating back thousands of years, through Egyptian, Greek, Persian and Roman history, the first libraries were primarily archives for storing information. As the majority of the population was illiterate during these eras, the knowledge stored was the preserve of the educated – the elite. However, when Gutenberg invented the printing press in the fifteenth century, books, literature, knowledge, became available to the masses. This was an epochal cultural movement that has evolved ever since – right up to the staggering speed of today's 'information society'.

Whereas the classical library was exclusive, and catered to the privileged classes, the modern library is inclusive and accommodates all social classes, genders and ages. Hence it is said that the library of the future will have to break down barriers further. This is an interesting task for the architect – to design a building that defies conventions and looks to the future.

As the function of the library has developed extensively, so too has the architecture. I believe that library architecture has evolved to represent a building typology of unique character, with huge social, educational, and cultural potential, and of great importance to the society of today and tomorrow.

The Modern Library

Why do people visit libraries in the first place? And what can the library offer nowadays, when information is accessible to almost everyone, anywhere, at any time?

The library is a public and social space, which, alongside museums, is one of the few existing non-commercial civic spaces available to us. At the library, knowledge is readily available to visitors who get the chance to use different sorts of media, more or ess free. At the library, we can avail of materials and services, and this should be considered an unconditional privilege.

The library of the future has to meet the individual user's specific needs, as well as the opposing needs for immersion and community. Users have a long list of diverse motivations for visiting the library; for example, the social dimension that lies in being surrounded by pecple. Moreover, users come to enlighten themselves with knowledge, to find information, to keep track of the flow of news; some do academic research, others get together with their study group or book club. A substantial proportion of users come to be seen in the city's cultural hot spot, to gain, and contribute to, so-called 'cultural capital'.

As libraries make knowledge and space available for the masses, they become the epitome of community spirit. One essential function of the modern library is to give access to media that will help people interpret and understand the world in which we live. For this reason, it is important to maintain the idea of the library as a place that represents democratic values, while offering a publicly available and social platform on which to act.

The Library as the Third Place

Libraries play an important role in society because they function as social hubs and urban meeting places. Consequently, when designing libraries, the architect holds, through the organisation of space, a unique opportunity to improve and create new ways for people to interact.

The theory of the 'Third Place' can explain why libraries are connected with this idea of social hubs. The concept was coined in 1989 by urban sociologist Ray Oldenburg, in his book *The Great Good Place*, in which a number of locations, outside of people's homes and workplaces, are analysed. From a theoretical perspective, the concept refers to informal places where people meet, in a community or neighbourhood, in order to build friendships, to discuss different subjects and to network. Third Places are valuable because they create space for human interaction, instilling the feeling of belonging and community, which can also be a source of pride. Moreover, Oldenburg finds that Third Places promote sociability while fighting isolation, because they make room for friendships and relaxation after a long day's work. In this way, Third Places become neutral ground – the intersection between the public and private spheres – where demands and obligations associated with work and family life are precluded. The library, as a positive example, offers an open and casual space between home and work.

Library architecture that expresses openness, accessibility and inclusiveness, connects to the ideas of the theory of the Third Place in interesting ways, as a space fulfilling defined and undefined needs. The library provides room for both formal and informal activities; on one hand, the specific physical environment attached to the library's functions and services, and, on the other, space for relaxing and interacting.

Designing the Modern Library

Today's digital and transformative society calls for access to relevant knowledge – fast. Therefore, the library of the future must meet users' expectations of twenty-four-hour access to knowledge. At the same time, the Internet and new media are challenging the position of the printed book, because they make for flexible alternatives, potentially changing users' expectations and behaviour. However, contrary to concerns that libraries might become redundant, their role and influence is likely to expand as the need for new adaptable and accessible learning spaces increases.

The library serves its patrons through the functionality and comfort of the interior environment – and yet it must aspire to an architectural identity of its own. Many aspects should be taken into consideration during the design phase of a library. If we are to aspire to design library architecture that will appear accessible, inclusive and open, the best way to achieve this is to ensure that the design process itself opens up and adapts to new ideas – for instance, by inviting user-groups to join in.

Dialogue and interaction with the future users of the building is a challenging but very valuable development tool for the architect – and the participatory process of user-driven design innovation can be integrated at the earliest stage to great advantage. The professional librarian, students, visitors, and surrounding community in general can contribute with rewarding ideas, input, and, most of all, specific knowledge. Moreover, this process creates an important sense of commitment and ownership.

User perspectives bring insight into work processes, work functions, work relations, visitor behaviour, service expectations, information requests – all of which outline the needs and priorities of future users and staff. The user-groups can be asked to relate to specific issues – the site, geometry and interior – and provide the design team with as much relevant information as possible.

Not only will user involvement in the design process stimulate and develop ownership and affiliation in the public at large, but the library architecture, when completed, will also communicate recognisable values for the institution, the city and the surrounding community.

Sense of Place

Most of us have been to a library, and we all have our own opinion on the library as institution and as place. The library as place is associated with different impressions retained by our senses – acoustics, silence, the scent of books, illumination, losing track of time. The library is ancient, it is iconic, but it is also a known place, an open institution, situated in the town in which you live, at the school or university where you study, or in the building you pass on your way to work. I like to refer to the characteristic atmosphere of the library as a 'sense of place'.

When places have been given a stronger meaning or definition by society, they are said to have a strong sense of place. Designing modern multifunctional libraries is all about creating unique places with a strong identity and character, connecting to the user's defined and undefined needs; places that foster a sense of authentic attachment and belonging.

Architecture is closely connected to the experience of sense of place, and will change by degrees. In contemporary and future society, the library as institution will indisputably play a rising and significant role. The library will continue to be a unique space for learning, sharing, and interacting, as well as a haven for immersion and inspiration. I cannot imagine a time where such a place will ever be expendable.

Vorwort

Bibliotheken als literarische oder filmische Schauplätze haben Kultcharakter. Sie werden häufig als mystische und geheimnisvolle Orte in Szene gesetzt, als düstere Stätten der Stille, an denen der Protagonist nach Antworten und Erkenntnissen sucht. Der Betrachter dekodiert und erkennt die konstruierte Abbildung einer Bibliothek als möglichen eigenen Bezugspunkt. Es ist faszinierend, wie die fiktionale Repräsentation einer Bibliothek häufig einen intensiven atmosphärischen, ja geradezu räumlichen Eindruck hinterlässt, während sie sich gleichzeitig vom selbsterworbenen Wissen des Betrachters von den Eigenschaften einer authentischen modernen Bibliothek unterscheidet.

Entstehung

Die Bibliothek als Institution existiert bereits seit dem Altertum. Vor Tausenden von Jahren dienten erste Vorläufer moderner Bibliotheken bei den Ägyptern, Griechen, Persern und Römern noch hauptsächlich als Archive zur Aufbewahrung von Wissen. Da der Großteil der einstigen Bevölkerung aber aus Ungebildeten bestand, blieb das verwahrte Wissen der gelehrten Elite vorbehalten. Bis Gutenberg im 15. Jahrhundert die Druckerpresse erfand und Bücher, Literatur, Wissen auch der breiten Masse zugänglich wurden. Diese epochale Kulturbewegung hat sich seither gehörig entwickelt – und im heutigen „Informationszeitalter" mächtig Fahrt aufgenommen.

Wo die Urbibliothek noch auf Exklusivität setzte und rein auf die privilegierten Klassen ausgerichtet war, steht die zeitgenössische Bibliothek Menschen aus allen Gesellschaftsschichten und unabhängig von Geschlecht oder Alter offen. Demzufolge werden zukünftige Bibliotheken der Beseitigung von Barrieren wohl noch mehr Bedeutung beimessen, was Architekten vor die faszinierende Aufgabe stellt, unkonventionelle und zukunftsgerichtete Gebäude zu entwerfen.

Mit der umfangreichen Entwicklung der Bibliotheksfunktion hat sich auch die Architektur selbst verändert. Meiner Meinung nach hat sich die Bibliotheksarchitektur in eine Richtung entwickelt, die die Darstellung einer einzigartigen und für die gegenwärtige wie auch die zukünftige Gesellschaft bedeutsamen Gebäudetypologie mit enormem sozialem, pädagogischem und kulturellem Potential in den Mittelpunkt stellt.

Die moderne Bibliothek

Warum besuchen Menschen überhaupt eine Bibliothek? Und was hat eine Bibliothek heute noch zu bieten, wo Information beinahe jedem Menschen überall und jederzeit zugänglich ist?

Bibliotheken sind öffentliche und soziale Räume, die neben Museen zu den wenigen gemeinnützigen gesellschaftlichen Räumen zählen, die uns zur Verfügung stehen. In der Bibliothek wartet Wissen in Form verschiedenster Medien bereitwillig nur darauf, von Besuchern erschlossen zu werden, und das noch dazu mehr oder weniger kostenlos. In der Bibliothek haben wir die uneingeschränkte Möglichkeit, Unterlagen und Dienste in Anspruch zu nehmen, was vorbehaltlos durchaus als Privileg betrachtet werden darf.

Die Bibliothek der Zukunft muss sowohl den besonderen Ansprüchen individueller Benutzer als auch den gegenläufigen Bedürfnissen nach Versenkung und Gemeinschaft genügen. Bibliotheksbenutzer suchen diese Horte des Wissens aus den verschiedensten Beweggründen auf: Beispielsweise der sozialen Komponente wegen, befinden sie sich in Bibliotheken doch in menschlicher Gesellschaft. Darüber hinaus möchten Benutzer natürlich auch ihren Horizont erweitern, Informationen finden, in Bezug auf Neuigkeiten auf dem Laufenden bleiben; so mancher forscht zu wissenschaftlichen Fragen, wieder andere treffen sich hier mit Kollegen aus ihrer Lerngruppe oder ihrem Buchklub. Daneben sucht ein erheblicher Teil der Benutzer diese städtische Kulturhochburg nur deshalb auf, um gesehen zu werden, sogenanntes „Kulturkapital" zu erwerben oder dieses zu mehren.

Bibliotheken bieten der breiten Masse Zugang zu Wissen und Raum und werden so zum Inbegriff von Gemeinschaftssinn. Eine zentrale Funktion moderner

Avant-propos

Littérature et cinéma ont souvent représenté la bibliothèque comme un lieu hautement symbolique du mystère et du secret où, plongé dans la pénombre et le silence, on y cherche des réponses, en quête du savoir ultime. L'archétype même de la bibliothèque évoque, par son interprétation, un lieu reconnaissable entre tous auquel quiconque peut se rattacher. Il est d'ailleurs intéressant de constater à quel point l'idée que l'on se représente de ce lieu exprime souvent une forte impression, une atmosphère typique, pourtant différente de l'expérience que procurent les bibliothèques modernes, bien réelles celles-ci.

Evolution

La bibliothèque en tant qu'institution trouve son origine dans l'antiquité. Vieilles de plusieurs millénaires, au temps des Egyptiens, des Grecs, des Perses et des Romains, les premières bibliothèques servaient alors d'archives permettant de conserver une trace écrite de l'information. La plupart de ces peuples ne sachant ni lire ni écrire, les connaissances ainsi accumulées étaient l'apanage des classes instruites, de l'élite. L'imprimerie, invention géniale de Gutenberg au quinzième siècle, a toutefois permis de vulgariser les œuvres, la littérature, et bien d'autres savoirs. Ce formidable tournant culturel, pour l'époque, a depuis cédé la place à notre « société de l'Information » et son culte de l'instantané.

Alors que la bibliothèque antique était réservée aux privilégiés, la bibliothèque moderne est ouverte à tous et accueille toutes les catégories sociales, genre et âge confondus. D'où l'affirmation que la bibliothèque de demain n'aura pas d'autres choix que d'éliminer les dernier obstacles à la connaissance. Quoi de plus exaltant pour un architecte que le défi d'imaginer un lieu à l'encontre de toute convention, tourné vers l'avenir ?

Si la bibliothèque voit sa fonction prendre une ampleur significative, il en va de même pour l'architecture. Le style architectural des bibliothèques s'est lui-même transformé pour adopter une typologie de construction singulière dont le rôle social, éducatif et culturel revêt une importance capitale pour les sociétés d'aujourd'hui et de demain.

La bibliothèque moderne

Pour quelle raison, essentielle, se rend-on à la bibliothèque ? Qu'a-t-elle à proposer en cette ère de l'information omniprésente à laquelle presque tout le monde a accès ?

Espace public et social, la bibliothèque, au même titre que le musée, est l'un des rares lieux citadins à vocation non commerciale qui s'offre à nous. La bibliothèque met à la disposition du visiteur, plus ou moins gracieusement, un véritable puits de connaissances pour peu qu'il sache manier différents supports. Pouvoir bénéficier des équipements et des services des bibliothèques est un privilège inconditionnel et doit continuer d'être considéré comme tel.

Si demain, la bibliothèque doit répondre aux attentes propres à chaque utilisateur, elle doit aussi satisfaire les besoins, pourtant contraires, d'immersion et d'appartenance communautaire. Les raisons qui poussent les visiteurs à se rendre à la bibliothèque sont aussi nombreuses que diverses, à l'instar par exemple, de la dimension sociale que revêt le fait d'être assis parmi d'autres personnes. Les utilisateurs y viennent par ailleurs pour se cultiver, se documenter ou se tenir informés ; certains y poursuivent leurs recherches universitaires, d'autres y retrouvent leur groupe de travail ou leur club de lecture. Un nombre important d'utilisateurs apprécient d'être vus dans ce qu'ils considèrent le carrefour culturel incontournable de la ville, pour profiter et apporter leur pierre à son fameux 'capital culturel'.

En rendant accessibles au grand public, connaissances et espaces, les bibliothèques incarnent la quintessence même de l'esprit de communauté. Une fonction essentielle de la bibliothèque moderne est de donner accès aux supports qui permettront aux visiteurs d'interpréter et de comprendre le monde dans lequel ils évoluent. Il est capital, pour cette raison, de conserver l'idée d'une bibliothèque garante des valeurs démocratiques, d'une plateforme grand public et interactive à dimension sociale.

Prólogo

Como escenografía literaria o fílmica, la biblioteca constituye todo un símbolo. A menudo, se representa como un lugar místico y secreto, como un espacio difuminado y silencioso, donde el protagonista va en busca de respuestas y de sabiduría. El espectador descodifica y reconoce la representación construida de la biblioteca como un lugar con el que se puede identificar. Resulta interesante ver cómo la representación imaginaria de la biblioteca suele crear un poderoso sentido de ambiente –un poderoso sentido territorial– a la vez que difiere del conocimiento que experimenta el espectador de la auténtica biblioteca de hoy en día.

Evolución

La biblioteca como institución data de los tiempos antiguos. Las primeras bibliotecas, que se remontan a miles de años, a lo largo de toda la historia egipcia, griega, persa y romana, fueron originalmente archivos para almacenar información. Como la mayoría de la población era analfabeta en esas épocas, el conocimiento almacenado era patrimonio de las clases cultas: la élite. Sin embargo, cuando Gutenberg inventó la imprenta en el siglo XV, los libros, la literatura y el conocimiento se fueron generalizando de forma masiva. Fue un movimiento cultural que hizo época y ha seguido evolucionando desde entonces hasta alcanzar una velocidad de vértigo en la «sociedad de la información» actual.

Mientras que la biblioteca clásica era exclusiva y se dirigía a las clases privilegiadas, la biblioteca moderna es integradora y acoge a todas las clases sociales, sexos y edades. Por lo tanto, se dice que la biblioteca del futuro tendrá que seguir rompiendo barreras. Ésta es una tarea llena de interés para el arquitecto: diseñar un edificio que desafíe las convenciones y mire hacia el futuro.

Del mismo modo que la función de la biblioteca se ha desarrollado considerablemente, así lo ha hecho también la arquitectura. Creo que la arquitectura de la biblioteca ha evolucionado hasta representar una tipología de edificio de carácter único, con un inmenso potencial social, educativo y cultural, de gran importancia para la sociedad actual y futura.

La biblioteca moderna

¿Por qué frecuenta la gente las bibliotecas en primer lugar? ¿Y qué pueden ofrecer las bibliotecas hoy en día, cuando la información está al alcance prácticamente de todos, en cualquier parte y en todo momento?

La biblioteca constituye un espacio público y social que, junto con los museos, es uno de los pocos espacios cívicos no comerciales existentes a nuestra disposición. En la biblioteca, el conocimiento siempre está disponible para los visitantes que tienen la oportunidad de utilizar distintos tipos de soportes, más o menos gratuitos. En la biblioteca, sacamos partido de materiales y servicios, lo que hay que considerar como un privilegio absoluto.

La biblioteca del futuro debe satisfacer las necesidades específicas del usuario individual, así como las exigencias contrapuestas de inmersión y comunidad. Los usuarios tienen una larga lista de motivaciones diversas para ir a una biblioteca; por ejemplo, la dimensión social que se plasma en el hecho de estar rodeados de gente. Por otra parte, los usuarios vienen a instruirse con el conocimiento, buscar información, seguir el hilo de las noticias; algunos realizan investigaciones académicas, otros se reúnen con su grupo de estudios o su club de lectura. Una parte sustancial de usuarios vienen a que les vean en el punto cultural más atractivo de la ciudad, para sacar partido y contribuir al llamado «capital cultural».

Como las bibliotecas ponen el conocimiento y el espacio a disposición de las masas, se convierten en la quintaesencia del espíritu comunitario. Una función esencial de la biblioteca moderna en la actualidad es proporcionar acceso a los medios de comunicación que ayudan a las personas a interpretar y comprender el mundo en el que vivimos. Por este motivo, es importante mantener la idea de que la biblioteca es un lugar que representa valores democráticos, a la vez que ofrece una plataforma social y accesible al público en la que actuar.

Bibliotheken besteht darin, Menschen Zugang zu Medien zu verschaffen, um ihnen die Deutung und das Verständnis der Welt zu erleichtern, in der wir alle leben. Aus diesem Grund ist es unabdingbar, die Auffassung von der Bibliothek als einem Ort demokratischer Werte aufrechtzuerhalten, der gleichzeitig eine öffentlich zugängliche und soziale Plattform bildet, die nutzbar gemacht werden kann.

Die Bibliothek als Dritter Ort

Bibliotheken spielen aufgrund ihrer Funktion als soziale Knoten- und urbane Treffpunkte eine gesellschaftlich bedeutende Rolle. Demzufolge bietet sich Architekten bei Entwürfen für Bibliotheken über das Element der Raumgestaltung bzw. -organisation eine einzigartige Gelegenheit zur Verbesserung und Erschaffung neuer Wege zwischenmenschlicher Interaktion.

Die Theorie des Dritten Ortes kann erklären, warum Bibliotheken mit der Idee sozialer Knotenpunkte eng verknüpft sind. Der Begriff wurde im Jahr 1989 vom Stadtsoziologen Ray Oldenburg in seinem Buch *The Great Good Place* geprägt, in dem eine Reihe von Orten abseits der Wohn- und Arbeitsstätten von Menschen einer Untersuchung unterzogen wurden. Aus einer theoretischen Perspektive betrachtet, bezieht sich dieses Konzept auf informelle Orte, an denen sich Menschen innerhalb einer Gemeinschaft oder Wohngegend treffen, um Freundschaften einzugehen, Verschiedenstes zu besprechen und Beziehungen zu pflegen. Dritte Orte sind deshalb von Bedeutung, weil sie Raum für zwischenmenschliche Interaktion schaffen und auf diese Weise für Zugehörigkeit und Gemeinschaft sorgen, was nicht zuletzt als Quelle für Selbstwertgefühl und Stolz fungieren kann. Darüber hinaus glaubt Oldenburg, dass Dritte Orte die Geselligkeit fördern und die Vereinsamung eindämmen, weil sie Freundschaften und ganz allgemein der Entspannung nach einem langen Arbeitstag den notwendigen Platz einräumen. Auf diese Weise werden Dritte Orte zu neutralem Boden – zum Schnittpunkt zwischen der öffentlichen und der privaten Sphäre – wo Forderungen und Verpflichtungen seitens der Arbeit oder der Familie keinerlei Rolle spielen. Als positives Beispiel bietet die Bibliothek einen offenen und ungezwungenen Raum zwischen Heim- und Arbeitsstätte.

Eine Bibliotheksarchitektur, die Offenheit, Zugänglichkeit und Einbeziehung ausdrückt, schlägt eine interessante Brücke zur Theorie der Dritten Orte und fungiert als Ort der Erfüllung genau festgelegter wie vollkommen diffuser Bedürfnisse gleichermaßen. Bibliotheken stellen Raum bereit, der sowohl für formelle als auch informelle Aktivitäten genutzt werden kann: Einerseits die einzigartigen, den Bibliotheksfunktionen und -diensten beigefügten räumlichen Besonderheiten, und andererseits der zur Entspannung und Interaktion dienende Raum.

Entwurf der modernen Bibliothek

Die digitale Transformationsgesellschaft unserer Zeit fordert Zugang zu relevantem Wissen, und das schnell. Aus diesem Grund werden zukünftige Bibliotheken nicht umhin können, den Anspruch ihrer Benutzer auf rund um die Uhr zugängliches Wissen zu erfüllen. Gleichzeitig stellen das Internet und die neuen Medien die Position des gedruckten Wortes immer weiter in Frage, indem sie für flexiblere Alternativen und für potentiell veränderte Erwartungshaltungen und Verhaltensweisen von Benutzern sorgen. Wie dem auch sei, entgegen Befürchtungen, wonach Bibliotheken überflüssig werden könnten, wird ihre Rolle und ihr Einfluss aufgrund der immer stärkeren Nachfrage nach anpassungsfähigen und zugänglichen Lernräumen wohl noch weiter zunehmen.

Bibliotheken dienen ihren Besuchern aufgrund der Funktionalität und des Komforts ihrer Innenräume – und müssen doch danach streben, eine eigene architektonische Identität auszubilden. Im Zuge der Planungsphase von Bibliotheken gilt es, zahlreiche unterschiedliche Aspekte in Betracht zu ziehen. In unserem Streben nach einer Bibliotheksarchitektur der Offenheit, Zugänglichkeit und

La bibliothèque comme « tiers lieu »

Véritables lieux d'échanges sociaux et de rencontres urbaines, les bibliothèques jouent un rôle essentiel dans la société. L'architecte chargé de concevoir une bibliothèque se voit ainsi offrir l'incroyable opportunité, à travers l'organisation de différents espaces, d'améliorer les possibilités d'interactions sociales, voire d'en créer de nouvelles.

C'est à la lumière de la théorie du « tiers lieu » que la bibliothèque prend tout son sens de carrefour social. Ce concept a été inventé en 1989 par le sociologue urbain Ray Oldenburg qui propose, dans son ouvrage intitulé *The Great Good Place*, une analyse d'un certain nombre de lieux, en dehors de la maison et du travail. D'un point de vue théorique, les tiers lieux désignent des endroits informels où l'on peut se réunir, au sein d'une communauté ou d'un quartier, pour nouer des amitiés, évoquer divers sujets ou élargir son réseau de connaissances. Les tiers lieux sont précieux en ce sens qu'ils aménagent des espaces propices aux interactions sociales, et suscitent un sentiment d'appartenance et d'adhésion communautaire, source supplémentaire de fierté. Oldenburg rajoute par ailleurs que les tiers lieux encouragent la sociabilité en combattant l'isolement, en tant que cadres d'échanges et de détente après une longue journée de travail. A cet égard, les tiers lieux s'érigent, à la croisée des sphères publiques et privées, en véritables terrains neutres dont sont exclues toute exigence ou autre obligation liée au travail ou au cadre familial. La bibliothèque illustre à merveille ce type de lieu avec ses espaces ouverts et informels qui trouvent naturellement leur place entre la maison et le travail.

Les bibliothèques, par leur architecture ouverte, accessible et accueillante, font écho de manière fort intéressante à la théorie du tiers lieu, tant elles répondent à des attentes aussi précises qu'elles peuvent être indéfinies. La bibliothèque est en effet le foyer d'activités à la fois formelles et informelles ; elle intègre, d'une part, l'environnement physique propre à ses fonctions et ses services, et fournit, d'autre part, un lieu de détente et d'interaction.

Concevoir la bibliothèque moderne

À l'ère du numérique et de la mutation, nos sociétés imposent un accès rapide à la somme de toutes les connaissances disponibles. La bibliothèque de demain doit donc répondre aux attentes des usagers qui veulent tout savoir tout de suite. Dans le même temps, Internet et les nouvelles technologies menacent le statut du livre en offrant des alternatives flexibles, elles-mêmes susceptibles de modifier les besoins et les comportements. Pour autant, loin des craintes de voir les bibliothèques tomber en désuétude, leur rôle et leur influence risquent au contraire de s'élargir face au besoin croissant pour de nouveaux espaces d'apprentissage modulables et accessibles.

Si la bibliothèque répond à son public avec un cadre intérieur fonctionnel et confortable, elle doit dans le même temps aspirer à une identité architecturale qui lui soit propre. De nombreux aspects entrent en jeu dans la phase conceptuelle d'un tel lieu. Si l'objectif est de construire une bibliothèque qui donne le sentiment d'être réellement accessible, accueillante et ouverte, la meilleure façon d'y parvenir est de s'assurer que le processus de conception soit lui-même ouvert et intègre les nouvelles idées. Solliciter l'avis de groupes d'utilisateurs est un exemple parmi d'autres de bonnes pratiques en la matière.

Initier le dialogue et échanger avec les futurs usagers du bâtiment peuvent certes relever d'un exercice périlleux pour l'architecte, mais combien précieux en phase de développement. Ce processus d'innovation conceptuelle participative, alimenté par les usagers, peut être mis en place à un stade précoce du projet, pour en tirer de plus grands bénéfices. Bibliothécaires professionnels, étudiants, visiteurs et communauté au sens large peuvent contribuer au projet en soumettant des idées et des opinons enrichissantes, et bien souvent en faisant profiter de leurs connaissances particulières. Pareille collaboration suscite en outre un fort sentiment d'adhésion et d'appartenance.

Les avis des usagers éclairent d'un nouveau regard les méthodes, les fonctions et les relations de travail, les

La biblioteca como tercer lugar

Las bibliotecas desempeñan una importante función en la sociedad porque actúan como centros sociales y puntos de encuentro urbanos. En consecuencia, al diseñar una biblioteca, el arquitecto tiene, gracias a la organización del espacio, una oportunidad única de mejorar y crear nuevas formas de interacción entre las personas.

La teoría del «Tercer Lugar» puede servir de explicación sobre por qué las bibliotecas están relacionadas con esta idea de centros sociales. El concepto lo acuñó en 1989 el sociólogo urbano Ray Oldenburg, en su libro *The Great Good Place*; en él analiza cierto número de sitios, excluidas las casas y los lugares de trabajo. Desde un punto de vista teórico, el concepto hace referencia a lugares informales donde las personas se reúnen, en una comunidad o un barrio, para crear amistades, debatir sobre distintos temas e interrelacionarse. Los terceros lugares son valiosos porque crean un espacio para la interacción humana, inculcando un sentimiento de pertenencia y comunidad, lo que puede ser igualmente motivo de orgullo. Asimismo, Oldenburg cree que los terceros lugares promueven la sociabilidad, a la vez que luchan contra el aislamiento, porque dejan espacio para la amistad y la relajación después de un largo día de trabajo. De este modo, los terceros lugares se convierten en espacios neutrales –la intersección entre las esferas pública y privada– donde las exigencias y obligaciones asociadas a la vida laboral y familiar quedan excluidas. La biblioteca, como ejemplo positivo, ofrece un espacio abierto e informal entre la casa y el trabajo.

La arquitectura de la biblioteca, que expresa transparencia, accesibilidad e integración, conecta con las ideas de la teoría del Tercer Lugar de diversas maneras, como espacio que satisface necesidades definidas e indefinidas. La biblioteca proporciona espacio tanto para actividades formales como informales; por una parte, el entorno físico específico reservado a las funciones y servicios de la biblioteca y, por otra, un espacio para la relajación y la interacción.

Diseño de la biblioteca moderna

La sociedad digital y en constante evolución de hoy en día exige un rápido acceso al conocimiento requerido. Por lo tanto, la biblioteca del futuro debe cumplir las expectativas de los usuarios de tener acceso al conocimiento las 24 horas del día. Al mismo tiempo, Internet y los nuevos medios de comunicación plantean un desafío a la posición del libro impreso porque ofrecen alternativas flexibles, lo que puede modificar a su vez las expectativas y el comportamiento de los usuarios. Sin embargo, contrariamente a la idea de que las bibliotecas puedan volverse superfluas, es probable que su función e influencia se expandan al ir aumentando la necesidad de contar con nuevos espacios de aprendizaje adaptables y accesibles.

La biblioteca da servicio a su público a través de la funcionalidad y comodidad de su ambiente interior y debe aspirar además a presentar una identidad arquitectónica propia. Se deben tener en cuenta numerosos aspectos durante la fase de diseño de una biblioteca. Si debemos aspirar a diseñar una arquitectura de biblioteca accesible, integradora y abierta, la mejor forma de lograrlo es garantizando que el proceso de diseño en sí se abra y adapte a nuevas ideas, por ejemplo, invitando a grupos y usuarios a que participen en él.

El diálogo y la interacción con los futuros usuarios del edificio constituye una herramienta de desarrollo que supone un reto pero es a la vez de gran valía para el arquitecto. La innovación del procedimiento participativo en el diseño basado en el usuario se puede integrar en el proceso en su fase más temprana, para mayor beneficio de todos. Los bibliotecarios profesionales, estudiantes, visitantes y la comunidad circundante en general pueden contribuir con ideas y aportaciones enriquecedoras y, por encima de todo, con un conocimiento específico. Asimismo, este proceso crea un importante sentido de compromiso y propiedad.

Los puntos de vista de los usuarios aportan mayores perspectivas sobre los procesos de trabajo, funciones laborales, relaciones laborales, comportamiento de visitantes,

Einbeziehung sollte möglichst auch der Entwurfsprozess selbst von Offenheit und Anpassungsfähigkeit an neue Ideen geprägt sein – indem beispielsweise Benutzergruppen dazu eingeladen werden, ihre Vorstellungen einzubringen.

Der Dialog und die Interaktion mit den zukünftigen Gebäudebenutzern stellt ein anspruchsvolles, aber äußerst lohnendes Entwicklungsinstrument für Architekten dar – und der Mitbestimmungsprozess benutzergesteuerter Designinnovationen kann bereits in die Frühphase des Prozesses integriert werden und tatsächlich entscheidende Vorteile nach sich ziehen. Bibliothekare, Studenten, Besucher sowie die umliegende Gemeinschaft ganz allgemein können über lohnende Ideen, Kritik und vor allem spezifisches Wissen ihren Beitrag leisten. Darüber hinaus führt diese Vorgehensweise zu Engagement und einem Gefühl der Eigenverantwortlichkeit.

Benutzerperspektiven ermöglichen Einsichten in Arbeitsprozesse, Arbeitsfunktionen, Arbeitsbeziehungen, Besucherverhalten, Erwartungshaltungen in Verbindung mit Dienstleistungen, Auskunftsansuchen, die allesamt Informationen zu den Bedürfnissen und Prioritäten zukünftiger Benutzer und Mitarbeiter liefern. Benutzergruppen können gebeten werden, auf ganz bestimmte Angelegenheiten Bezug zu nehmen – die Anlage, die Gestaltung oder das Interieur – und dem Entwurfsteam möglichst viele relevante Informationen zukommen zu lassen.

Die Einbeziehung von Benutzern in den Entwurfsprozess wird nicht nur ganz allgemein zur Förderung und Entwicklung eines Gefühls von Eigenverantwortung und Zugehörigkeit in der Öffentlichkeit führen, sondern über die vollendete Bibliotheksarchitektur zudem wiedererkennbare Werte für die Institution, die Stadt und die umliegende Gemeinschaft vermitteln.

Raumempfinden

Die meisten von uns waren bereits das eine oder andere Mal in einer Bibliothek und wir alle vertreten eigene Ansichten zur Bibliothek als Institution und als Ort. Bibliotheken als Orte stehen mit unterschiedlichen Eindrücken in Verbindung, die uns unsere Sinne vermitteln – Klänge, Stille, der Geruch von Büchern, Beleuchtung, Verlust des Zeitgefühls. Bibliotheken sind altertümliche Orte mit Kultcharakter und gleichzeitig vertrautes Terrain und offene Einrichtungen der eigenen Stadt, der eigenen Schule, der eigenen Universität oder innerhalb eines Gebäudes unweit des eigenen Arbeitsplatzes. Das charakteristische Ambiente von Bibliotheken bezeichne ich gerne als „Raumempfinden".

Orte, die innerhalb einer Gesellschaft eine größere Bedeutung oder genauere Abgrenzung erlangt haben, gelten gemeinhin als Orte mit intensivem „Raumempfinden". Moderne Multifunktionsbibliotheken zu entwerfen bedeutet, einzigartige Orte mit ausgeprägter Identität und starkem Charakter zu erschaffen, die sich der genau festgelegten wie der vollkommen diffusen Bedürfnisse von Benutzern annehmen; es geht um Orte, die das Gefühl echter Verbundenheit und Zugehörigkeit stärken.

Architektur ist aufs engste mit der Erfahrung des Raumempfindens verbunden und wandelt sich schrittweise. In der Gesellschaft von heute sowie jener von morgen werden Bibliotheken als Institutionen zweifelsfrei eine immer bedeutendere und zentrale Rolle spielen. Sie werden auch weiterhin einzigartige Orte des Lernens, Teilens und der zwischenmenschlichen Interaktion sein sowie Horte der Versenkung und Inspiration. Ich kann mir kein Zeitalter vorstellen, das auf solche Orte verzichten könnte.

comportements des visiteurs, les attentes liées aux services, les demandes d'informations, etc., autant de facteurs qui mettent en avant les nouveaux besoins et les priorités des utilisateurs et du personnel de demain. Il est ainsi possible de sonder des groupes d'utilisateurs autour de thématiques spécifiques comme le choix du site, la géométrie et le cadre intérieur, et de fournir à l'équipe de conception le plus d'informations pertinentes possible.

Placer l'usager au cœur du processus de conception contribuera à stimuler et à renforcer le sentiment d'appartenance et d'adhésion chez le grand public, relayé dans l'architecture même de la bibliothèque qui, une fois achevée, véhiculera des valeurs reconnaissables pour l'institution, la ville et la communauté tout entière.

S'imprégner de l'atmosphère du lieu

Nous avons tous, à un moment donné, côtoyé une bibliothèque. Cette institution et le cadre qui la caractérise ne laissent personne indifférent. En tant que lieu, la bibliothèque réveille diverses impressions gardées en mémoire par nos sens : l'acoustique, le silence, l'odeur des livres, l'éclairage, la perte de la notion de temps. Ancestrale, hautement symbolique, la bibliothèque n'en demeure pas moins un repère connu de tous, une institution ouverte indissociable de la ville où vous habitez, de l'école ou de l'université que vous fréquentez, du trajet pour se rendre au travail. J'aime à comparer cette ambiance si caractéristique que dégage la bibliothèque à cette notion 'd'atmosphère, d'impression du lieu'.

Ne dit-on pas d'un lieu chargé de sens ou lourd de signification qu'il dégage une vive « impression », une « atmosphère » particulière ? Concevoir des bibliothèques modernes aux fonctions multiples revient à imaginer des lieux uniques dotés d'une forte identité, mais toujours en rapport avec les attentes précises, et celles moins définies des utilisateurs ; des lieux auxquels on est véritablement attaché, qui appartiennent à la collectivité.

Étroitement liée à cette impression d'atmosphère du lieu, l'architecture opèrera une transformation progressive. Dans nos sociétés contemporaines et celles en devenir, la bibliothèque en tant qu'institution est incontestablement amenée à jouer un rôle grandissant et significatif, sans cesser d'incarner cet espace unique d'apprentissage, de partage et d'interaction, ainsi que ce havre d'immersion et d'inspiration. Je n'ose imaginer que pareille institution soit un jour appelée à disparaître.

expectativas de servicio, solicitudes de información, todo lo cual perfila las necesidades y prioridades de los futuros usuarios y empleados. Se puede pedir a grupos y usuarios que se relacionen con cuestiones específicas –el centro, la geometría y el interior– y proporcionen al equipo de diseño la mayor información posible.

No solo la implicación de los usuarios en el proceso de diseño estimulará y desarrollará el sentido de propiedad y afiliación en el público en general, sino que la arquitectura de la biblioteca, una vez finalizada, transmitirá igualmente valores reconocibles para la institución, la ciudad y la comunidad circundante.

Sentido de lugar

La mayoría de nosotros ha estado en una biblioteca y tenemos nuestra propia opinión de la biblioteca como institución y como lugar. La biblioteca como lugar está asociada a distintas impresiones conservadas por nuestros sentidos: acústica, silencio, olor de los libros, iluminación, pérdida de la noción del tiempo. La biblioteca es antigua, emblemática pero es también un lugar conocido, una institución abierta, situada en la ciudad en la que vive, en la escuela o la universidad en la que estudia o en el edificio junto al que pasa de camino al trabajo. Me gusta hacer referencia al ambiente tan característico de la biblioteca como «sentido de lugar».

Cuando la sociedad ha otorgado a los lugares un marcado significado o definición, se dice que desprenden un fuerte «sentido de lugar». El diseño de modernas bibliotecas multifuncionales se basa en la creación de lugares únicos con un marcado carácter e identidad, relacionados con las necesidades definidas e indefinidas del usuario; lugares que promueven un sentido auténtico de apego y pertenencia.

La arquitectura está estrechamente relacionada con la experiencia del sentido de lugar y irá cambiando gradualmente. En la sociedad contemporánea y futura, la biblioteca como institución desempeñará irrefutablemente una función significativa y creciente. La biblioteca seguirá siendo un lugar único para el aprendizaje, el uso compartido y la interacción, así como un refugio para la inmersión y la inspiración. No me puedo imaginar una época en la que un lugar así pueda llegar a ser prescindible.

Library of Alexandria

Alexandria, Egypt
Snøhetta, 2002

The ancient Library of Alexandria dominated the classical world of learning, and the new library, standing on roughly the same site, has similarly lofty ambitions. From above, it takes the shape of a simple circle, suggesting the all-powerful sun, but in height, it goes from 15.8 metres underground to 37 metres above ground, tilting towards the sea. The main reading room cascades over eleven levels, where slender columns support the roof and its skylights. Externally, the granite walls are carved with characters from over one hundred different human scripts, calling to mind the universal influence of the library's predecessor.

Im Altertum beherrschte die antike Bibliothek von Alexandria die Welt des Wissens und die neue, unweit der historischen Stätte errichtete Bibliothek hat sich ähnlich hochfliegende Ziele gesteckt. Aus der Vogelperspektive betrachtet gleicht ihre Form einem schlichten Kreis, was als Anspielung auf die allmächtige Sonne zu verstehen ist, während sie in der Vertikalen von 15,8 m unter der Erdoberfläche auf stattliche 37 m darüber aufragt und sich gleichzeitig dem Meer zuneigt. Der kaskadenartig abfallende Hauptleseraum nimmt sage und schreibe elf Stockwerke ein und das Dach mit seinen Oberlichten wird von schlanken Säulen getragen. Die granitenen Außenmauern zieren Zeichen aus über hundert verschiedenen menschlichen Schriften und gemahnen an den universellen Einfluss der einstigen Urbibliothek.

Si l'antique Bibliothèque d'Alexandrie dominait en son temps le monde de la connaissance, le nouvel édifice, qui s'élève approximativement sur le même site, entend poursuivre les mêmes nobles objectifs. Vu d'en haut, l'édifice dévoile une forme circulaire épurée qui rappelle la toute-puissance du soleil. Toutefois, le bâtiment, incliné en direction de la mer, s'enfonce à 15,8 mètres sous le sol et s'élève 37 mètres au-dessus du sol. La salle de lecture principale se déploie en cascade sur onze niveaux, où de fines colonnes supportent le toit et ses puits de lumière. Au-dehors, plus d'une centaine de signes humains ont été gravés sur les murs en granit pour rappeler le rayonnement universel de son illustre ancêtre.

La antigua Biblioteca de Alejandría dominaba el mundo clásico de los conocimientos y la nueva biblioteca, que se erige aproximadamente en el mismo lugar, exhibe las mismas elevadas ambiciones. Desde arriba, presenta la forma de un simple círculo que sugiere el sol todopoderoso, pero su altura alcanza desde los 15,8 metros por debajo de tierra hasta los 37 metros por encima, inclinándose hacia el mar. La sala de lectura principal cae en cascada sobre once niveles, en ella esbeltas columnas soportan el techo y sus claraboyas. En el exterior, en los muros de granito están tallados los caracteres de más de un centenar de escrituras humanas distintas, que evocan la influencia universal del predecesor de la biblioteca.

ГОСУДАРСТВЕННАЯ БИБЛИОТЕКА СССР имени «ЛЕНИНА»

Russia's largest library, and one of the largest in the world, began life in 1862, as the library division of the Moscow Public Museum and Rumyantsev Museum. In 1925, it was renamed for Lenin and became the country's national library. Its collection had been developing rapidly, and when it outgrew the prestigious Pashkov House, overlooking the Kremlin, plans were drawn up for the imposing building we see today. Construction was a lengthy process; it was designed in 1927, work began in 1930, and although largely complete in 1941, it was developed and extended as recently as 1960. It was renamed the Russian State Library in 1992.

Russian State Library

Moscow, Russia
Vladimir Shchuko & Vladimir Gelfreikh, 1941

La mayor biblioteca de Rusia, y una de las más grandes del mundo, comenzó su andadura en 1862 como biblioteca del Museo Público de Moscú y del Museo Rumiántsev. En 1925, fue rebautizada con el nombre de Lenin y se convirtió en la biblioteca nacional del país. Su colección se desarrolló con gran rapidez y, al superar la capacidad de la prestigiosa Casa Pashkov, frente al Kremlin, se procedió a planificar la imponente biblioteca que admiramos hoy en día. Su construcción implicó un largo proceso: fue diseñada en 1927, las obras comenzaron en 1930 y, aunque finalizaron en gran medida en 1941, se siguió desarrollando y ampliando en una época tan reciente como 1960. Fue rebautizada como Biblioteca Estatal de Rusia en 1992.

Russlands größte Bibliothek ist gleichzeitig eine der größten Büchersammlungen der Welt und wurde im Jahr 1862 als Bibliothek des Öffentlichen Museums Moskaus und des Rumjanzew-Museums begründet. 1925 wurde sie in Leninbibliothek umbenannt und diente unter dieser Bezeichnung als Nationalbibliothek des Landes. Als das prestigeträchtige und den Kreml überragende Paschkow-Haus dem rasch wachsenden Bibliotheksbestand nicht mehr genügte, entstanden die Pläne für das imposante gegenwärtige Gebäude, dessen Errichtung jedoch sehr viel Zeit in Anspruch nahm: Der Baubeginn des 1927 entworfenen Gebäudes erfolgte im Jahr 1930 und obwohl das Gebäude 1941 größtenteils vollendet war, wurde es noch bis ins Jahr 1960 verändert bzw. erweitert. Seit 1992 trägt die Einrichtung den Namen Russische Staatsbibliothek.

Plus grande bibliothèque de Russie, et l'une des plus grandes du monde, l'édifice fut inauguré en 1862 en tant que division du Musée public de Moscou et du Musée Roumiantsev. C'est en 1925, après avoir été renommée en l'honneur de Lénine, que la bibliothèque a acquis son statut de bibliothèque nationale du pays. Surplombant le Kremlin, la prestigieuse Maison Pachkov, qui abritait alors la Bibliothèque, ne suffisant plus à abriter la collection, victime de son développement fulgurant, il fut décidé de concevoir les plans de l'imposant bâtiment que nous connaissons aujourd'hui. Projet de longue haleine, l'édifice fut conçu en 1927, mais sa construction ne débuta qu'en 1930. Bien que quasiment achevée en 1941, la Bibliothèque fut encore développée et agrandie au début des années 60. Elle fut enfin rebaptisée Bibliothèque d'Etat de Russie en 1992.

King Fahd National Library

Riyadh, Saudi Arabia
Eckhard Gerber, 2013

Commissioned by the Kingdom of Saudi Arabia, the aim of this library was to create an iconic building that would reflect a forward-thinking and culturally astute nation. The bright, Bauhaus design was inspired by the traditional idea of the veiled woman; the suggestion that something of value must be elevated and protected. The new library surrounds its predecessor, a forty-year-old conventional edifice with domed roof, which now houses the archives. The symbol of the veil is echoed in the outer textile membrane, a nod to tradition which also protects the library from the effects of sandstorms and extreme heat.

Diese Bibliothek wurde vom Königreich Saudi-Arabien in dem Bestreben in Auftrag gegeben, einer zukunftsgerichteten und kulturell ausgereiften Nation ein ikonisches Baudenkmal zu setzen. Der heitere Bauhaus-Entwurf inspiriert sich an der traditionellen Auffassung von der verschleierten Frau und mithin der Ansicht, dass Wertvollem Verherrlichung und Schutz gebührt. Die neue Bibliothek wurde um ein herkömmliches, vier Jahrzehnte altes Vorgängergebäude mit Kuppeldach errichtet, in dem sich heute die Archive befinden. Das Schleiermotiv setzt sich in der textilen Außenmembran fort, die nicht nur auf das kulturelle Erbe der Bibliothek verweist, sondern diese auch vor den Auswirkungen von Sandstürmen und extremer Hitze schützt.

Le Royaume d'Arabie saoudite a commandé cette bibliothèque dans le but de se doter d'un monument emblématique, à l'image d'une nation avant-gardiste à la culture brillante. De style bauhausien, l'architecture lumineuse s'inspire largement de l'image traditionnelle de la femme voilée, dans l'idée de chérir et de protéger les trésors de la vie. La nouvelle bibliothèque encercle le précédent édifice conventionnel vieux de quarante ans avec son toit en dôme, qui abrite désormais les archives. Le symbole du voile se retrouve dans la membrane extérieure en textile, autre clin d'œil à la tradition, qui offre également à la bibliothèque une barrière contre les tempêtes de sable et la chaleur extrême.

El objetivo de esta biblioteca, realizada por encargo del Reino de Arabia Saudí, era crear un edificio emblemático que reflejara la visión de futuro y la apertura cultural de la nación. El ingenioso diseño Bauhaus se inspiró en la idea tradicional de la mujer con velo, sugiriendo que lo valioso se ha de elevar y proteger. La nueva biblioteca rodea a su predecesora, un edificio cuadragenario de factura convencional, con una cúpula en el techo, que ahora alberga los archivos. El símbolo del velo se traduce en la membrana textil que recubre el edificio, una alusión a la tradición que, además, protege a la biblioteca de los efectos de las tormentas de arena y del calor excesivo.

LiYuan Library

Jiaojiehe, Beijing, China
Li Xiaodong Atelier, 2011

In den Bergen vor den Toren Jiaojiehes befindet sich die auf den ersten Blick recht bescheidene LiYuan Library. Der Innenraum jedoch bietet durch die Verwendung von Stufen und unterschiedlichen Ebenen ein maximales Raumangebot und lockt mit so manch abgeschiedener Nische. Beeindruckende Fenster setzen friedvolle Panoramen gekonnt in Szene, während das für die Außenfassade verwendete Material das Licht dämpft und für behaglichen Lesegenuss sorgt. Nach der Fertigstellung wurde der ortsansässigen Gemeinde die Zusammenstellung des Bibliotheksbestandes übertragen, welche die Räumlichkeiten sogleich als Plattform für den Austausch von Ideen für sich entdeckte. Bislang verzeichnet die Sammlung über siebentausend Bücher und es steht zu erwarten, dass ihre Außenhülle aus unbehandelten Zweigen zu gegebener Zeit der lokalen Tier- und Pflanzenwelt als Refugium dienen wird.

D'apparence modeste, la bibliothèque Li Yuan se niche dans les montagnes autour du village de Jiaojiehe. A l'intérieur, divers jeux de marches et de niveaux optimisent l'espace en aménageant plusieurs alcôves. Les imposantes parois vitrées offrent une vue apaisante, la lumière naturelle filtrée par la structure extérieure invitant au plaisir de la lecture. Lors de la construction, la mise en place du fonds de la bibliothèque a été confiée à la communauté locale, érigeant le lieu en véritable plateforme d'échanges instantanés. La bibliothèque a reçu à ce jour plus de sept mille ouvrages. Revêtue de fines branches non traitées, la bibliothèque ne devrait pas tarder à abriter fleurs et autre faune sauvage.

In the mountains outside Jiaojiehe sits the seemingly modest LiYuan Library. Internally, steps and levels have been used to maximise space and create hideaways. Impressive windows frame peaceful views, and the external material tempers the light to allow for comfortable reading. Upon construction, it was down to the local community to build the library's collection, and it was an instant platform for exchanging ideas. It has received more than 7,000 books to date and, clothed as it is in untreated twigs, it is expected that flora and fauna will join the library in due course.

En las montañas de las afueras de Jiaojiehe, se encuentra la aparentemente modesta Biblioteca de LiYuan. En el interior, se han utilizado escalones y niveles para aumentar al máximo el espacio y crear ambientes aislados. Unas imponentes ventanas sirven de marco a unas vistas apacibles. El material empleado en el exterior atenúa la luz, lo que propicia una cómoda lectura. Tras su construcción, la comunidad local se encargó de constituir la colección de la biblioteca, que se convirtió de inmediato en una plataforma para el intercambio de ideas. Hasta la fecha, ha recibido más de 7.000 libros. Con su atavío de ramitas sin tratar, se espera que, con el tiempo, la flora y la fauna se sumen a la biblioteca.

The curved walls and elegant arches of Hachioji Library are in fact more influenced by nature than by classical architecture. Inspired by caves, the exterior, with its glass arches of varying spans, welcomes the natural surroundings into the neutral interior space, creating a suitably stimulating environment for students of art. Standing at two storeys over a basement, the first floor features an all-purpose gallery space and theatre area, and its concrete floor slopes down gently from the front entrance. The second floor accommodates the book stacks, and here, in contrast, the ceiling tilts up slightly, filling the reading areas with light.

Die geschwungenen Wände und eleganten Gewölbe der Hachioji-Bibliothek entspringen vielmehr der Natur selbst als einzelnen Formen klassischer Architektur. Ihr durch Höhlen inspiriertes Äußeres mit seinen Glasbögen unterschiedlicher Spannweiten bringt die natürliche Umgebung in den neutralen Innenraum, wodurch eine für Kunststudenten angemessen anregende Umgebung geschaffen wird. Der zweigeschossig über dem Parterre aufragende erste Stock verfügt über eine Allzweck-Galerie sowie einen Theaterbereich und der Betonboden fällt am Eingangsbereich beginnend sanft nach unten ab. Die Bücherregale befinden sich im zweiten Stock, dessen Decke wiederum geringfügig nach oben geneigt ist, wodurch der Lesebereich mit Licht durchflutet wird.

Les murs incurvés et les élégantes arches de la bibliothèque de Hachioji s'inspirent davantage de la nature que de l'architecture classique. A l'instar d'une grotte, l'extérieur, avec ses arches vitrées de diverses longueurs, donne sur un écrin de verdure qui s'invite tout naturellement dans un espace intérieur neutre, pour créer un environnement idéalement stimulant pour les étudiants en art. La bibliothèque s'élève sur deux niveaux. Le premier abrite une galerie à usages multiples, ainsi qu'un théâtre. L'entrée principale s'ouvre quant à elle sur un sol de béton en pente douce. Réservé aux livres, le second niveau contraste avec un plafond légèrement incurvé vers le haut qui inonde de lumière les espaces de lecture.

Hachioji Library

Tama Art University, Hachioji, Tokyo, Japan
Toyo Ito, 2007

Las paredes curvas y los elegantes arcos de la Biblioteca de Hachioji están realmente más influidos por la naturaleza que por la arquitectura clásica. Inspirado en las cuevas, el exterior, con sus arcos acristalados de distintas envergaduras, acoge los entornos naturales en el espacio interior neutral, lo que crea un ambiente estimulante muy adecuado para los estudiantes de arte. El primer piso, situado en dos plantas sobre un sótano, presenta un espacio multifuncional de galería y un área teatral. Su suelo de hormigón se inclina suavemente hacia abajo desde la entrada principal. La segunda planta aloja las estanterías de libros y, aquí, en contraste, el techo se inclina hacia arriba ligeramente, inundando de luz las zonas de lectura.

State Library of Victoria

Melbourne, Australia
Joseph Reed, 1856

Au nombre des premières biblio-thèques publiques libres du monde, la Bibliothèque d'Etat du Victoria s'est considérablement développée depuis sa création, et se compose désormais de vingt-trois bâtiments. L'édifice compte parmi ses pièces les plus emblématiques la salle de lecture Redmond Barry (1886), du nom de son fondateur, ainsi que la salle de lecture à coupole (1913). Cette dernière, conçue par Norman G. Peebles, s'inspire du Panthéon de Rome. Avec ses six niveaux, elle était alors considérée comme un véritable bijou architectural, une étiquette dont elle jouit toujours un siècle plus tard.

Die Staatsbibliothek von Victoria war eine der ersten unentgeltlichen öffentlichen Bibliotheken überhaupt. Die Einrichtung wurde seit ihrem Bestehen fortwährend und umfangreich ausgebaut und umfasst heute ganze 23 Gebäude. Zu den Glanzstücken zählen der nach seinem Stifter benannte Redmond-Barry-Lesesaal (1886) sowie der Kuppelsaal aus dem Jahr 1913, der von Norman G. Peebles entworfen und vom Pantheon im antiken Rom inspiriert wurde. Bei seiner Errichtung galt dieses sechsstöckige Gebäude als architektonisches Juwel und hat auch eineinhalb Jahrhunderte später nichts von seiner Faszination eingebüßt.

One of the first free public libraries in the world, the State Library of Victoria has been extensively developed since its foundation, and now comprises twenty-three buildings. Highlights include the Redmond Barry Reading Room (1886), which was named after its founder, and the Domed Reading Room (1913). The latter, designed by Norman G. Peebles, was inspired by the Pantheon in Rome. At six storeys, it was considered an architectural marvel, and remains so a century later.

Una de las primeras bibliotecas públicas gratuitas del mundo, la Biblioteca Estatal de Victoria ha experimentado un considerable desarrollo desde su fundación e incluye ahora veintitrés edificios. Entre sus elementos más destacados se encuentran la Sala de Lectura Redmond Barry (1886), que lleva el nombre de su fundador, y la Sala de Lectura Abovedada (1913). Ésta última, diseñada por Norman G. Peebles, se inspiró en el Panteón de Roma. Con sus seis plantas, estaba considerada como una maravilla arquitectónica y aún lo sigue siendo un siglo después.

State Library of Victoria, Melbourne, Australia

Designed with growth and changing reading habits in mind, the eleven-storey Seattle Central Library has a dynamic presence. With space for more than 1.45 million volumes, it is divided into five platforms and four flowing connecting planes, which vary in dimensions according to function and give the building its distinctive shape. The relaxed 'Living Room', for reading and using Wi-Fi, contrasts with the innovative non-fiction 'Books Spiral', which reasserts the Dewey Decimal System and arranges the ever-growing collection in a continuous ribbon. On the top floor, the reading room offers views of Puget Sound and the surrounding mountains.

Seattle Central Library

Seattle, Washington, USA
OMA/LMN, 2004

Das elfstöckige Gebäude der Seattle Central Library wurde mit Blick auf zukünftiges Wachstum und sich verändernde Lesegewohnheiten entworfen, was die Dynamik seiner Präsenz erklärt. Die Bibliothek ist für die Aufbewahrung von über 1,45 Millionen Artikeln ausgelegt und besteht aus fünf Plattformen sowie vier fließenden Verbindungsebenen, deren Dimensionen je nach Funktion variieren, was dem Bauwerk seine eigenwillige Form verleiht. Das zwanglose „Wohnzimmer" ist dem Schmökern und der Benutzung drahtlosen Internets gewidmet und hebt sich von der innovativen „Sachliteratur-Schnecke" ab, welche die unablässig wachsende Sammlung ganz im Sinne der Dewey-Dezimalklassifikation von Bibliotheksbeständen in einem fortlaufenden Band anordnet. Der Lesesaal im obersten Stockwerk bietet Aussichten auf die Meerenge des Puget Sound und die umliegenden Berge.

Pensée en fonction des nouvelles habitudes de lecture en plein développement, la Bibliothèque centrale de Seattle, avec ses onze niveaux, occupe l'espace de manière particulièrement dynamique. Pouvant accueillir jusqu'à 1,45 million de volumes, l'édifice se divise en cinq plateformes reliées entre elles par quatre niveaux suspendus dont les dimensions varient selon la fonction, conférant au bâtiment sa forme si particulière. Destinée à la lecture et à l'utilisation du Wi-Fi, la « Salle de séjour » dans un style décontracté, offre un contraste saisissant avec la « Spirale des livres » innovante et non-fictionnelle, qui réinterprète la Classification décimale de Dewey et organise la collection sans cesse grandissante en un ruban ininterrompu. A l'étage supérieur, la Salle de lecture offre un aperçu du détroit de Puget et des montagnes alentours.

La Biblioteca Central de Seattle, de once plantas, se diseñó teniendo en cuenta las costumbres de lectura cambiantes y crecientes, por lo que desprende una presencia dinámica. Con cabida para más de un millón cuatrocientos cincuenta mil volúmenes, está dividida en cinco plataformas y cuatro planos flotantes interconectados, que varían en dimensiones según su función y otorgan al edificio su forma característica. El relajante «Salón», para lectura y uso de Wi-Fi, contrasta con la innovadora «Espiral de libros» de no ficción, que reafirma el sistema de clasificación decimal de Dewey y organiza la creciente colección en una cinta continua. En la planta superior, la sala de lectura ofrece vistas del estrecho de Puget y de los montes del entorno.

José Vasconcelos Library

Mexico City, Mexico
Alberto Kalach, 2006

This library was intended to be the cornerstone of a literacy campaign, leading to a cultural and urban regeneration, and this objective permeates the structure. Conceived as a 'coffer of books', the narrow building is surrounded by botanical gardens which muffle urban noise and provide an interesting textural contrast to the concrete exterior. Internally, a network of stacks is suspended in a five-storey glass case, confronting the visitor with all the information available. Gabriel Orozco's sculpture 'Ballena', the skeleton of a grey whale, reinforces the ambitious scale of the project, which has room for a collection triple its current size.

Diese Bibliothek wurde als Eckpfeiler einer Alphabetisierungskampagne entworfen, die zu einer kulturellen wie urbanen Erneuerung führen soll, was sich wie ein roter Faden durch das gesamte Gebäudekonzept zieht. Das schmale und in Form einer „Bücherkiste" gehaltene Bauwerk ist von botanischen Gärten umgeben, die den Lärm der umliegenden Stadt dämpfen und einen spannenden strukturellen Kontrapunkt zum Beton der Außenfassade setzen. Im Inneren des Gebäudes enthält ein fünfgeschossiger Glaskasten ein hängend angebrachtes Geflecht aus Bücherregalen, das Besucher gleichsam mit der Gesamtheit des vorhandenen Wissens konfrontiert. Gabriel Orozcos gebührend „Ballena" genannte Skulptur eines Grauwalgerippes unterstreicht die ambitionierten Größenverhältnisse dieses Projekts, in dem bis zu drei Mal größere Sammlungen mühelos untergebracht werden könnten.

Pierre angulaire d'une vaste campagne d'alphabétisation, cette bibliothèque avait vocation à revitaliser le cadre culturel et urbain de la ville, des objectifs qui transparaissent dans sa structure. Conçue comme un véritable 'coffre à livres', l'édifice étroit s'élève au beau milieu de jardins botaniques qui étouffent le bruit de la ville et offrent un contraste contextuel intéressant avec l'extérieur bétonné de la bibliothèque. A l'intérieur, tout un réseau de bibliothèques suspendues dans un bloc de verre de cinq étages confronte le visiteur à l'incroyable quantité d'informations disponibles. La sculpture signée Gabriel Orozco 'Ballena', qui représente l'ossature d'une baleine grise, fait écho aux dimensions ambitieuses du projet, destiné à accueillir une collection pouvant atteindre trois fois sa taille actuelle.

Esta biblioteca estaba prevista que fuera la piedra angular de una campaña para la alfabetización que llevaría a una regeneración cultural y urbana, y este objetivo queda reflejado en la estructura. Diseñado para ser un «cofre de libros» el estrecho edificio está rodeado de jardines botánicos que atenúan el ruido urbano y proporcionan un interesante contraste de texturas al exterior de hormigón. En el interior, una red de estanterías suspendidas en una caja de cristal de cinco pisos enfrenta al visitante a toda la información disponible. La escultura de Gabriel Orozco «Ballena», el esqueleto de una ballena gris, refuerza las ambiciosas proporciones del proyecto, que tiene espacio para una colección que triplique su tamaño actual.

José Vasconcelos Library, Mexico City, Mexico

Library of Congress, Thomas Jefferson Building

Washington DC, USA
Paul J. Pelz & John L. Smithmeyer,
Edward Pearce Casey, 1897

The largest library in the world, with over 155 million volumes, the Library of Congress was established in 1800. It was housed in the Capitol until 1814, when invading British troops set fire to the building. When the small library was destroyed, retired President Thomas Jefferson offered his personal library as a replacement. In 1886, Congress finally authorised construction of a new Beaux-Arts-style library. In 1892, Casey took over supervision of the interiors, which included the work of more than fifty American artists. The Great Hall and the circular reading room are particularly representative of the library's importance.

Die im Jahr 1800 gegründete Kongressbibliothek ist mit über 155 Millionen Einträgen die größte Bibliothek der Welt. Bis 1814 war sie im Kapitol untergebracht, das jedoch von einfallenden Truppen der Briten in Brand gesteckt wurde. Der ehemalige Präsident Thomas Jefferson bot daraufhin seine Privatbibliothek als Ersatz für die durch das gelegte Feuer zerstörte kleine Bibliothek an. Im Jahr 1886 bewilligte der Kongress schließlich die Errichtung einer neuen Bibliothek im Stil des Historismus. 1892 wurde Casey die Aufsicht über das mit Arbeiten von über 50 amerikanischen Künstlern versehene Interieur übertragen. Insbesondere die Great Hall sowie der kreisrunde Lesesaal zeugen von der Bedeutung dieser Bibliothek.

Plus grande bibliothèque au monde, avec plus de 155 millions de volumes, la Bibliothèque du Congrès date de 1800. Elle était installée au Capitole jusqu'en 1814, année durant laquelle elle fut envahie par les troupes britanniques qui mirent feu au bâtiment et détruisirent la modeste bibliothèque. L'ancien Président Thomas Jefferson offrit alors de la remplacer par sa collection personnelle. En 1886, le Congrès finit par autoriser la construction d'une nouvelle bibliothèque de style Beaux-Arts. En 1892, Casey prit la direction des intérieurs auxquels ont contribué plus de cinquante artistes américains. Le Grand Hall et la Salle de lecture circulaire sont particulièrement représentatifs de l'importance de cette bibliothèque.

La Biblioteca del Congreso, la mayor biblioteca del mundo con más de 155 millones de volúmenes, fue fundada en 1800. Estuvo alojada en el Capitolio hasta 1814, cuando las tropas británicas invasoras prendieron fuego al edificio. Al destruirse la pequeña biblioteca, el presidente retirado Thomas Jefferson ofreció su biblioteca personal en sustitución. En 1886, el Congreso autorizó finalmente la construcción de una nueva biblioteca de estilo Beaux-Arts. En 1892, Casey organizó la supervisión del interior, que incluía el trabajo de más de cincuenta artistas americanos. El gran vestíbulo y la sala de lectura circular son especialmente representativos de la importancia de la biblioteca.

Library of Congress, Thomas Jefferson Building, Washington DC, USA

George Peabody Library

Johns Hopkins University, Baltimore, Maryland, USA
Edmund G. Lind, 1878

In 1857, Massachusetts-born philanthropist George Peabody dedicated the Peabody Institute to the citizens of Baltimore in appreciation of their hospitality. It is now part of Johns Hopkins University, but in accordance with Peabody's original gift, the library remains open to the general public. Described by the first Peabody provost, Nathaniel H. Morison, as a 'cathedral of books', it is renowned for its striking neo-Grec interior. The reading room features a bright atrium bordered by five tiers of elaborate cast-iron balconies, which rise dramatically to the highly lavish skylight, 19 metres above the black and white marble floor.

Im Jahr 1857 stiftete der aus Massachusetts gebürtige Philanthrop George Peabody das nach ihm benannte Peabody Institute den Bürgern von Baltimore, um sich für deren Gastfreundschaft erkenntlich zu zeigen. Zwar gehört es heute zur Johns-Hopkins-Universität, entsprechend Peabodys ursprünglicher Schenkung steht die Bibliothek jedoch auch weiterhin der Allgemeinheit offen. Das von Nathaniel H. Morison, dem ersten Leiter des Instituts, als „Kathedrale der Bücher" beschriebene Gebäude ist berühmt für sein markantes Interieur in neogriechischem Stil. Im Lesesaal befindet sich das helle Atrium, das von fünf Geschossen meisterlich ausgeführter Balkone aus Gusseisen umrahmt wird, die zum aufwendig gestalteten Oberlicht emporragen, das sich in beinahe 20 Meter Höhe über dem schwarz-weißen Marmorfußboden befindet.

En 1857, le philanthrope originaire du Massachusetts George Peabody dédia l'Institut Peabody aux citoyens de Baltimore en remerciement de leur hospitalité. L'institut fait désormais partie de l'Université Johns Hopkins, mais selon la volonté initiale de Peabody, la bibliothèque reste ouverte au grand public. Décrite par le premier prévôt de Peabody, Nathaniel H. Morison, comme une 'cathédrale de livres', la bibliothèque est célèbre pour son remarquable intérieur de style néo-grec. La Salle de lecture abrite un atrium lumineux bordé sur cinq niveaux de balcons travaillés en fer forgé, qui s'élèvent de manière spectaculaire jusqu'à la somptueuse verrière culminant à presque 19 mètres au-dessus du sol en marbre noir et blanc.

En 1857, el filántropo nacido en Massachusetts George Peabody dedicó el Instituto Peabody a los ciudadanos de Baltimore en agradecimiento a su hospitalidad. Ahora forma parte de la Universidad Johns Hopkins pero de acuerdo con la ofrenda original de Peabody, la biblioteca sigue abierta al público en general. Descrita por el primer rector de Peabody, Nathaniel H. Morison, como una «catedral de libros», es célebre por su llamativo interior neogriego. La sala de lectura presenta un atrio luminoso rodeado de cinco niveles de intrincadas galerías de hierro fundido, que surgen de forma espectacular hacia la suntuosísima claraboya, 19 metros por encima del suelo de mármol blanco y negro.

Biblioteca España

Medellín, Colombia
Giancarlo Mazzanti, 2007

The latter half of the twentieth century was a very turbulent time for Medellín, but since the death of Pablo Escobar it has been working to regain its reputation. Situated in the underprivileged Santo Domingo Savio barrio, the Parque Biblioteca España is a striking expression of this strength and determination. The three boulder-like buildings are linked by a concrete podium at the main level, and the window groupings are small and irregular in order to disconnect visitors from the world outside. The library is hugely popular with children, and has instilled a sense of pride in a most deprived area.

Die zweite Hälfte des 20. Jahrhunderts war für Medellín eine äußerst turbulente Zeit, seit dem Tod Pablo Escobars hat die Stadt jedoch vieles unternommen, um ihr einstiges Ansehen wiederzuerlangen. Die im unterprivilegierten Elendsbarrio von Santo Domingo Savio gelegene Parque Biblioteca España veranschaulicht diese Stärke und Entschlossenheit auf eindrucksvolle Weise. Die drei an Felsbrocken erinnernden Gebäude sind auf Höhe der Hauptebene durch eine Betonplattform verbunden und verfügen über kleine, unregelmäßige Fensterflächen, um Besucher die Außenwelt vorübergehend vergessen zu lassen. Die Bibliothek erfreut sich vor allem bei Kindern größter Beliebtheit und erfüllt eine der am meisten benachteiligten Gegenden der Stadt mit einem Gefühl von Stolz.

Biblioteca España, Medellín, Colombia

La dernière moitié du vingtième siècle a été une période très trouble pour Medellín, mais depuis la mort de Pablo Escobar, la ville œuvre à rétablir sa réputation. Situé dans le quartier défavorisé de Santo Domingo Savio, le « Parque Biblioteca España » (Parc de la bibliothèque Espagne) est une expression surprenante de cette force et de cette détermination. Les trois bâtiments qui rappellent des rochers sont reliés entre eux par une plateforme de béton au niveau principal du complexe, alors que les amas de fenêtres, petites et irrégulières, déconnectent le visiteur du monde extérieur. La bibliothèque rencontre un grand succès auprès des enfants, et suscite un certain sentiment de fierté dans une région particulièrement défavorisée.

En la segunda mitad del siglo XX, Medellín pasó por una época muy turbulenta, pero desde la muerte de Pablo Escobar se ha esforzado por recuperar una buena reputación. Situado en el desfavorecido barrio de Santo Domingo Savio, el Parque Biblioteca España constituye una llamativa expresión de esta energía y determinación. Los tres edificios, en forma de roca lisa, están unidos por un podio de hormigón en el nivel principal. Los grupos de ventanas son pequeños e irregulares para desconectar a los visitantes del mundo exterior. La biblioteca es muy popular entre los niños y ha inculcado un sentimiento de orgullo en un área muy desfavorecida.

New York Public Library,
Stephen A. Schwarzman Building

New York, USA
Carrère & Hastings, 1911

The first director of the New York Public Library, Dr John Shaw Billings, had a clear vision for a monumental but efficient building: a rectangular reading room over seven storeys of book stacks, which would allow for the rapid delivery of books. Costing $9 million, and taking nine years to construct, it is considered to be New York's most successful Beaux-Arts building. Two marble lions, Patience and Fortitude, stand guard at the austere and imposing façade, and in 1998 the iconic Rose Main Reading Room, with space for 700 readers, was restored to its original splendour.

Dr. John Shaw Billings, der erste Direktor der New York Public Library, verfolgte eine klare Vision für ein sowohl monumentales als auch effizientes Gebäude, das aus einem rechteckigen Lesesaal über sieben Stockwerken aus Bücherregalen bestehen sollte, um eine rasche Bereitstellung von Büchern zu ermöglichen. Die Bauzeit dieses neun Millionen Dollar teuren Gebäudes, das als New Yorks gelungenstes Beispiel für Beaux-Arts-Architektur gilt, betrug neun Jahre. Zwei marmorne Löwen, die Geduld und Tapferkeit symbolisieren, halten vor der strengen und imposanten Fassade Wache. Im Jahr 1998 wurde dem ikonischen Rose-Lesesaal, der 700 Lesern Platz bietet, sein ursprünglicher Glanz wiedergegeben.

New York Public Library, Stephen A. Schwarzman Building, New York, USA

Le premier directeur de la *New York Public Library*, Dr. John Shaw Billings, avait imaginé un bâtiment monumental mais efficace : une salle de lecture rectangulaire au-dessus de sept niveaux de magasins pour une remise rapide des livres. Ayant coûté 9 millions de dollars et bâti en neuf ans, l'édifice est considéré comme un chef-d'œuvre architectural du style Beaux-Arts à New York. Deux lions en marbre, Courage et Patience, montent la garde à l'entrée d'une façade austère et imposante. En 1998, après avoir été restaurée, l'emblématique Salle de lecture rose, pouvant accueillir jusqu'à 700 lecteurs, a retrouvé sa splendeur d'antan.

El primer director de la Biblioteca Pública de Nueva York, el Dr. John Shaw Billings, tenía una visión clara de un edificio monumental pero eficiente: una sala de lectura rectangular sobre siete plantas de estanterías de libros, que permitiese un rápido reparto de los libros. Con un coste de 9 millones de dólares y una construcción que duró nueve años, está considerado como el edificio de estilo Beaux-Arts más logrado de Nueva York. Dos leones de mármol, la Paciencia y la Fortaleza, hacen guardia en la austera e imponente fachada y en 1998 la emblemática sala de lectura, con espacio para 700 lectores, recuperó su esplendor original gracias a una restauración.

New York Public Library, Stephen A. Schwarzman Building, New York, USA

Royal Portuguese Reading Room

Rio de Janeiro, Brazil
Rafael da Silva e Castro, 1888

Founded in 1837 by a group of immigrants to promote culture among the Portuguese community in the then capital of the Empire, the current library was inaugurated in 1888. The neo-Manueline building evokes the exuberant era of Portuguese discovery, and the limestone façade, inspired by the Jerónimos Monastery, was carved in Lisbon and brought by ship to Rio de Janeiro. The neo-Manueline style continues inside, with ornamental doors and shelves, and numerous nods to the great writers and explorers of Portugal. The beautiful chandelier and iron skylight feature of the reading room was the first of its kind in Brazil.

Der *Königliche Lesesaal für portugiesische Literatur* wurde im Jahr 1837 von einer Gruppe Einwanderer mit der Absicht gegründet, der Kultur innerhalb der portugiesischen Gemeinschaft der damaligen Hauptstadt des Reiches einen größeren Stellenwert einzuräumen. Die bestehende Bibliothek wurde schließlich 1888 eröffnet. Das Gebäude im neo-manuelinischen Stil spielt auf die reiche und prosperierende Ära der portugiesischen Entdeckungen an und die vom Jerónimos-Kloster inspirierte Kalksteinfassade entstand in Lassabon, bevor sie auf dem Seeweg nach Rio de Janeiro gelangte. Auch das Gebäudeinnere präsentiert sich mit seinen Dekortüren und Bücherregalen im Stil der Neo-Manuelinik und verewigt zahlreiche große portugiesische Schriftsteller und Entdecker. Der wunderschöne Kronleuchter sowie die eiserne Oberlichtkonstruktion im Lesesaal waren die ersten ihrer Art in Brasilien.

Fondée en 1837 par un groupe d'immigrants désireux de promouvoir la culture au sein de la communauté portugaise dans la capitale de l'époque de l'Empire, la bibliothèque actuelle a été inaugurée en 1888. L'édifice de style néo-manuélin rappelle l'âge d'or des grandes découvertes portugaises. La façade en calcaire, directement inspirée du Monastère des Hiéronymites, a été sculptée à Lisbonne et transportée par bateau jusqu'à Rio de Janeiro. Le style néo-manuélin se prolonge à l'intérieur de la bibliothèque bardée de portes et d'étagères ornementales, et truffée de références aux grands écrivains et explorateurs portugais. Le magnifique lustre et la lucarne en fer forgé de la Salle de lecture furent les premiers du genre au Brésil.

Fundada en 1837 por un grupo de inmigrantes para fomentar la cultura entre la comunidad portuguesa en la entonces capital del imperio, la biblioteca actual se inauguró en 1888. El edificio neomanuelino evoca la época exuberante del descubrimiento portugués y la fachada de piedra caliza, inspirada en el Monasterio de los Jerónimos, se esculpió en Lisboa y se transportó en nave a Río de Janeiro. El estilo neomanuelino se prolonga en el interior, con puertas y estanterías ornamentados, y numerosos bustos de grandes escritores y exploradores portugueses. El magnífico detalle de la araña y la claraboya de hierro de la sala de lectura fue el primero de su género en Brasil.

TEA includes a public library, an art museum, and several spaces for the community. Accessible from all sides, and intersected by a public path, everything about the building beckons the outside world in. Its two storeys are connected by a sweeping spiral staircase, and the modern lighting features provide a refreshing contrast to the dark concrete, which calls to mind the volcanic rock of Tenerife. Externally, there are 1,200 small glazed openings which during the day are reminiscent of the sun shimmering on the sea, and at night animate the skyline, making the library a vibrant Santa Cruz landmark.

Der TEA umfasst eine öffentliche Bibliothek, ein Kunstmuseum und mehrere, der Gemeinschaft zur Verfügung stehende Räume. Alles an diesem von allen Seiten zugänglichen und durch einen öffentlichen Weg unterteilten Gebäude fordert die Außenwelt zum Eintritt auf. Eine ausladende Wendeltreppe verbindet die beiden Geschoße des TEA und die modernen Beleuchtungselemente bilden einen erfrischenden Kontrast zum dunklen Beton, der Teneriffas Vulkangestein nachahmt. Die Außenfassade wird durch 1200 kleine verglaste Öffnungen durchbrochen, die tagsüber an das auf den Meereswellen glitzernde Sonnenlicht erinnern, und nachts die Skyline zum Leben erwecken und die Bibliothek in ein pulsierendes Wahrzeichen der Stadt Santa Cruz verwandeln.

TEA Tenerife Arts Space

Santa Cruz de Tenerife, Canary Islands, Spain
Herzog & de Meuron, 2008

Le TEA abrite une bibliothèque publique, un musée d'art et plusieurs espaces communautaires. Accessible de toutes parts, et entrecoupé d'une allée publique, tout dans cet édifice invite le monde extérieur à pénétrer dans ses lieux. Les deux niveaux du complexe sont reliés par un large escalier en spirale, et l'éclairage moderne offre un contraste agréable avec le béton de couleur sombre, qui évoque la roche volcanique de Ténériffe. La façade extérieure, composée de 1 200 minuscules baies vitrées, rappelle, le jour, les reflets du soleil sur la mer, et anime, la nuit venue, l'horizon, faisant de cette bibliothèque un carrefour incontournable de Santa Cruz.

TEA incluye una biblioteca pública, un museo de arte y varios espacios para la comunidad. Accesible por todas partes y atravesado por una vía pública, todo en este edificio invita a adentrarse en él al mundo exterior. Sus dos plantas están conectadas por una escalera en espiral de gran amplitud y las modernas funciones de iluminación proporcionan un contraste refrescante con el hormigón oscuro, que recuerda la roca volcánica de Tenerife. En el exterior, 1.200 pequeños orificios acristalados recuerdan, de día, el sol resplandeciendo en el mar y, de noche, animan la línea del horizonte. Todo esto convierte la biblioteca en un punto de referencia vibrante de Santa Cruz.

Joanina Library

University of Coimbra, Coimbra, Portugal
Gaspar Ferreira, 1728

The University of Coimbra, the only ancient university in Portugal, was founded in 1290 and originally located in Lisbon. It was rebuilt in Coimbra in the eighteenth century by King João V, whose reign brought renewed prosperity to the country. His coat of arms is visible above the great portico at the entrance. The library's thick walls and doors help to protect its 250,000 volumes from the heat and humidity. Practicality aside, the interiors of the three-storey library are richly Baroque, with gilded detailing, rich wood and painted ceilings running through its three great rooms.

Die im Jahre 1290 ursprünglich in Lissabon gegründete Universität Coimbra ist die einzige Universität Portugals aus dieser Epoche. König Johann V., dessen Regierungszeit dem Land erneut Wohlstand brachte, ließ sie im 18. Jahrhundert in Coimbra wiedererrichten. Sein Wappen krönt den großen Portikus im Eingangsbereich. Die dicken Mauern und Türen der Bibliothek schützen die hier gelagerten 250.000 Artikel vor Hitze und Feuchtigkeit. Von diesem eher praktischen Aspekt abgesehen, präsentiert sich das Interieur der drei Haupträume der dreistöckigen Bibliothek mit seinen vergoldeten Verzierungen sowie üppigen und bisweilen bemahlten Holzdecken überaus barock.

Fondée en 1290, l'Université de Coimbra, la plus ancienne du Portugal, était initialement située à Lisbonne. Elle fut reconstruite à Coimbra au dix-huitième siècle par le Roi Jean V du Portugal, sous le règne duquel le pays renoua avec la prospérité. Son armoirie trône au-dessus du grand portique à l'entrée. Les murs épais et les lourdes portes de la bibliothèque protègent les 250 000 volumes qu'elle abrite de la chaleur et de l'humidité. Indépendamment de ces considérations pratiques, les trois vastes niveaux de la bibliothèque sont richement décorés dans le style baroque, que viennent sublimer des dorures, de somptueuses boiseries et des peintures au plafond.

La Universidad de Coimbra, la única universidad antigua de Portugal, se fundó en 1290 y, en su origen, se encontraba en Lisboa. En el siglo XVIII, el rey Juan V, cuyo reinado aportó una renovada prosperidad al país, la volvió a construir en Coimbra. Su escudo está visible en la parte superior del gran pórtico de la entrada. Los gruesos muros y puertas de la biblioteca ayudan a proteger sus 250.000 volúmenes contra el calor y la humedad. Aspectos prácticos aparte, el interior de la biblioteca de tres plantas es de un estilo barroco suntuoso, con elementos dorados, maderas preciadas y techos pintados a lo largo de sus tres grandes salas.

National Library of Ireland

Dublin, Ireland
Thomas Deane, 1890

The National Library of Ireland was established in 1877, and the present building was opened in 1890. Since then it has been extended, in keeping with its classical style, and today it is a reference library with upwards of 8 million items, including artefacts from some of Ireland's most revered writers. It has a bright and welcoming atmosphere, and an array of rich decorative elements. The horseshoe-shaped reading room, with its central dome and cherub frieze, is a particular highlight.

Fondée en 1877, la *National Library of Ireland* n'a ouvert physiquement ses portes qu'en 1890. Depuis, le bâtiment a connu plusieurs extensions, toujours dans le prolongement de son style classique. La bibliothèque est aujourd'hui une institution de référence avec une collection de plus de 8 millions d'ouvrages qui inclut les œuvres de certains des écrivains irlandais parmi les plus populaires. Le bâtiment dégage une atmosphère lumineuse et accueillante, magnifiée par de somptueux éléments décoratifs, dont la pièce maîtresse, avec son dôme central et sa frise de chérubins, est la salle de lecture en forme de fer à cheval.

La Biblioteca Nacional de Irlanda se fundó en 1877 y el edificio actual se inauguró en 1890. Desde entonces se ha ido ampliando aunque sin renunciar a su estilo clásico. En la actualidad, se considera una biblioteca de referencia con más de 8 millones de artículos, incluidas pertenencias de algunos de los escritores más venerados de Irlanda. Ofrece un ambiente luminoso y acogedor, así como una serie de suntuosos elementos decorativos. Destaca, en particular, la sala de lectura en forma de herradura, con la cúpula central y el friso de querubines.

Die Irische Nationalbibliothek wurde im Jahr 1877 gegründet und das auch heute noch genutzte Gebäude 1890 eröffnet. Seither wurde es unter Berücksichtigung seines klassischen Stils erweitert und die Irische Nationalbibliothek gilt heute mit über acht Millionen Einträgen und so manchem Artefakt von einigen der angesehensten Schriftsteller Irlands zurecht als Referenzbibliothek. Die Bibliothek verfügt über ein helles und einladendes Ambiente und zahlreiche aufwendige Zierelemente. Der hufeisenförmige Leseraum samt zentraler Kuppel und Cherub-Fries stellt ein besonderes Kleinod dar.

National Library of Ireland, Dublin, Ireland

Trinity College Library

Dublin, Ireland
Thomas Burgh, 1732

Trinity College Dublin was established in 1592, and its library is the largest in Ireland. The 65-metre library known as the 'Long Room' is perhaps most famous for two very precious manuscripts, the Book of Kells and the Book of Durrow, both of which it received in the 1660s. In 1801, it became a legal deposit library, and so in 1860 the flat ceiling was replaced with timber tunnel vaults to provide more space for the growing collection. The Long Room is now a sanctuary for 200,000 antique volumes, and it welcomes approximately half a million visitors every year.

Das Dubliner Trinity College wurde im Jahr 1592 gegründet und beherbergt Irlands größte Bibliothek. Ihren Ruf verdankt die auch als ‚Langraum' bekannte, 65 Meter lange Bibliothek in erster Linie wohl zwei überaus wertvollen Manuskripten: Dem Book of Kells und dem Book of Durrow, die dem Bibliotheksbestand in den 1660er-Jahren hinzugefügt wurden. Im Jahr 1801 wurde sie zu einer Pflichtexemplarbibliothek umgewandelt, weshalb ihre flache Decke 1860 durch hölzerne Tunnelgewölbe ersetzt wurde, um genügend Platz für den stetig wachsenden Bestand zur Verfügung zu stellen. Der Langraum ist heute ein Hort für 200.000 antike Bände und heißt jährlich ungefähr eine halbe Million Besucher willkommen.

Le Trinity College de Dublin a été fondé en 1592, et sa bibliothèque est la plus grande d'Irlande. Longue de 65 mètres, la 'Long Room' (salle oblongue) tire sans doute son prestige des deux précieux manuscrits qu'elle abrite : le Livre de Kells et le Livre de Durrow, tous deux acquis par la bibliothèque dans les années 1660. En 1801, l'établissement fut proclamé bibliothèque de dépôt légal, raison pour laquelle le plafond plat fut remplacé, en 1860, par des voûtes cintrées en bois pour aménager davantage d'espace à la collection grandissante. La *Long Room* est désormais le sanctuaire de 200 000 ouvrages antiques et accueille près d'un demi-million de visiteurs chaque année.

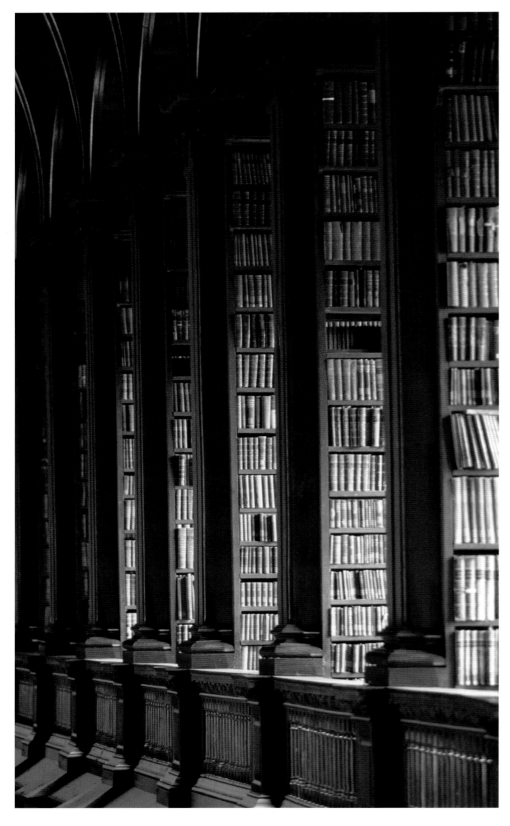

El Trinity College de Dublín se fundó
en 1592 y su biblioteca es la más
grande de Irlanda. La biblioteca de
65 metros conocida como la «Sala
Larga» debe posiblemente su fama
a dos manuscritos muy valiosos: el
Libro de Kells y el Libro de Durrow,
que pasaron ambos a formar parte
de la biblioteca en la década de 1660.
En 1801, se convirtió en una biblioteca
de depósito legal y en 1860, el techo
plano fue sustituido por una bóveda
de cañón de madera, lo que proporcionó
más espacio para la creciente colección.
La Sala Larga, actualmente un refugio
para 200.000 volúmenes antiguos,
recibe aproximadamente medio millón
de visitantes al año.

Trinity College Library, Dublin, Ireland

Glasgow School of Art Library

Glasgow, Scotland
Charles Rennie Mackintosh, 1909

Situated at the edge of a steep south-facing hill, the Glasgow School of Art is an eclectic mix of Scottish Baronial, Art Nouveau and modern influences, but its best-known interior is undoubtedly its library. Standing at two storeys, with a mezzanine overlooking the first floor, the room's abundance of dark wood makes it appear larger. Although this was his first major commission, Mackintosh confidently plays with Arts and Crafts ideals, and all the furniture and fixtures, including the eye-catching pendant lights on black chains, are painted and pierced with Art Nouveau motifs.

Wiewohl die am Rande eines steilen Südhangs erbaute Glasgow School of Art das Produkt einer eklektischen Mischung aus Schottischem Baronialstil, Jugendstil und modernen Einflüssen ist, bleibt ihr bekanntestes Merkmal wohl zweifelsohne ihre Bibliothek. Das gerade einmal zweistöckige Gebäude, dessen Parterre von einem Mezzanin überragt wird, wirkt aufgrund der üppigen Verwendung von dunklen Holzelementen größer, als es tatsächlich ist. Obwohl es sich dabei um seinen ersten Großauftrag überhaupt handelte, spielte Mackintosh selbstsicher mit Idealen der Arts-and-Crafts-Bewegung. Sämtliche Möbel und Einrichtungsgegenstände, darunter die auffälligen, an schwarzen Ketten hängenden Pendelleuchten, sind mit Jugendstilmotiven bemahlt und geschmückt.

Située en haut d'une colline à pente abrupte exposée plein sud, la *Glasgow School of Art* frappe par son association d'influences éclectiques puisant tour à tour dans le style des demeures seigneuriales écossaises, dans l'art nouveau et l'architecture moderne. L'élément le plus célèbre du bâtiment reste cependant la bibliothèque qu'il abrite. Construite sur deux niveaux, avec une mezzanine surplombant le premier étage, la salle, caractérisée par l'abondance de boiseries sombres, semble beaucoup plus grande. Bien que l'édifice ait été sa première œuvre majeure, Mackintosh n'a pas hésité à jouer des codes des Arts et Métiers. L'ensemble du mobilier et des matériels, y compris les remarquables luminaires suspendus à des chaînes noires, sont peints et truffés de motifs d'Art Nouveau.

Situada al borde de una empinada colina orientada hacia el sur, la Escuela de Arte de Glasgow presenta una combinación ecléctica de influencias modernas, Art Nouveau y señoriales escocesas, pero su interior más conocido es sin duda alguna la biblioteca. Ubicada en dos plantas, con un altillo que domina el primer piso, la abundancia de madera oscura de la sala le confiere mayor amplitud. Aunque éste fue su primer encargo importante, Mackintosh juega, lleno de confianza, con los ideales del movimiento Arts and Crafts, y todos los muebles y elementos fijos, incluidas las vistosas luces que cuelgan de cadenas negras, están pintados y perforados con motivos Art Nouveau.

Library of El Escorial

San Lorenzo de El Escorial, Madrid, Spain
Juan Bautista de Toledo, Juan de Herrera, 1592

Inscrit au patrimoine mondial de l'UNESCO, l'Escurial est la résidence historique du Roi d'Espagne, et abrite également un monastère, un musée et une école. Philippe II (1527–1598) a légué l'intégralité de sa collection personnelle à la bibliothèque, qui abritait durant son règne une salle tout entière dédiée aux manuscrits anciens en langue latine, grecque, arabe et espagnole, dont certains ouvrages confisqués pendant l'Inquisition. Malgré une façade extérieure sobre, les cinq salles de la bibliothèque richement décorées de marbre et de dorures rappellent le Siècle d'or espagnol, notamment les fresques de Pellegrino Tibaldi, représentations allégoriques des arts libéraux.

Now a UNESCO World Heritage site, El Escorial is a historical residence of the King of Spain, and also a monastery, museum and school. Philip II (1527–1598) donated his entire collection to the library, and during his reign there was an entire room dedicated to ancient manuscripts in such languages as Latin, Greek, Arabic, and Spanish, including books confiscated during the Inquisition. Despite the exterior's sober façade, the interiors of the library's five rooms are rich with marble, gilding, and nods to Spain's Golden Age, particularly Pellegrino Tibaldi's frescoes, which are allegorical depictions of the liberal arts.

El Escorial, que forma parte del Patrimonio de la Humanidad de la UNESCO, es una residencia histórica del Rey de España, así como un monasterio, un museo y una escuela. Felipe II (1527–1598) donó su colección completa a la biblioteca y durante su reinado, había toda una sala dedicada a manuscritos antiguos en idiomas como latín, griego, árabe y español, incluidos libros confiscados durante la Inquisición. A pesar de la sobria fachada exterior, el interior de las cinco salas que componen la biblioteca es suntuoso y está decorado con mármoles, dorados y bustos del Siglo de Oro español. Destacan, en particular, los frescos de Pellegrino Tibaldi: unas representaciones alegóricas de las artes liberales.

Die geschichtsträchtige einstige Residenz des Königs von Spanien, zu der außerdem ein Kloster, ein Museum und eine Schule gehören, ist heute eine UNESCO-Weltkulturerbestätte. Philip II. (1527–1598) vermachte der Bibliothek seine gesamte Sammlung und während seiner Regentschaft war ein ganzer Raum eigens nur für Manuskripte in lateinischer, griechischer, arabischer und spanischer Sprache vorgesehen, darunter auch von der Inquisition beschlagnahmte Werke. Im Gegensatz zur schlichten Außenfassade des Gebäudes spielen die fünf prunkvoll mit Marmor und Vergoldungen gestalteten Innenräume der Bibliothek auf die Glanzzeit Spaniens an, allem voran Pellegrino Tibaldis Fresken in Form allegorischer Abbildungen der freien Künste.

Sir Duncan Rice Library

University of Aberdeen, Scotland
schmidt hammer lassen architects, 2012

Established in 1495, the University of Aberdeen is the fifth oldest English-language university in the world. In 2012, the Sir Duncan Rice Library was opened. It was inspired by 'the ice and light of the north', as is evident in its clean and shimmering façade. Internally, a vast atrium with sweeping asymmetric contours connects its eight generously day-lit storeys, which house 13 kilometres of bookshelves and offer splendid views across the city.

Sir Duncan Rice Library, University of Aberdeen, Scotland

Die 1495 gegründete Universität Aberdeen ist die fünftälteste englischsprachige Universität der Welt. Im Jahr 2012 wurde die Sir-Duncan-Rice-Bibliothek eröffnet, die vom „Eis und Licht des Nordens" inspiriert wurde, wie sich an ihrer glatten und schimmernden Fassade unschwer ablesen lässt. Im Gebäudeinneren verbindet ein weitläufiges Atrium mit ausladenden asymmetrischen Konturen die acht lichtdurchfluteten Stockwerke, die Bücherwände mit einer Gesamtlänge von 13 km beherbergen und atemberaubende Aussichten über die Stadt ermöglichen.

Fondée en 1495, l'Université d'Aberdeen est la cinquième plus ancienne université anglophone du monde. La Bibliothèque Sir Duncan Rice a ouvert ses portes en 2012. Avec sa façade épurée aux reflets chatoyants, le bâtiment affiche clairement le parti pris de l'architecte de rappeler 'la glace et la lumière typique du Nord'. L'intérieur s'organise autour d'un vaste atrium aux larges contours asymétriques qui assure la liaison entre les huit étages généreusement baignés de lumière abritant 13 kilomètres de rayonnages, et offre un magnifique aperçu de la ville.

Fundada en 1495, la Universidad de Aberdeen es la quinta universidad de habla inglesa más antigua del mundo. En 2012, se inauguró la Biblioteca Sir Duncan Rice. Se inspiró en «la luz y el hielo del norte», tal y como lo demuestra su fachada nítida y reluciente. En su interior, un atrio espacioso, con unas curvas asimétricas de gran amplitud, conecta sus ocho plantas generosamente iluminadas con luz natural. En ellas se alojan 13 kilómetros de estanterías de libros y se ofrecen unas vistas espléndidas de la ciudad.

Europe's largest public library, overlooks Centenary Square in the heart of Birmingham. Its gold, silver and glass façade is clad with thousands of linking metal rings that represent the city's famous jewellery quarter and industrial origins. Internally, a staggered rotunda, crowned by the Shakespeare Memorial Room, forms the core of eight circular spaces. Along with three main reading rooms, a children's library, galleries and cafés, it has a rooftop garden and an external sunken amphitheatre. Described by the architect as a 'people's palace', it has been designed to accommodate an expected 3 million visitors per year.

Wuchtig ragt Europas größte öffentliche Bibliothek über dem im Herzen Birminghams gelegenen Centenary Square auf. Ihre aus Gold, Silber und Glas bestehende Fassade setzt sich aus tausenden miteinander verbundenen Metallringen zusammen, die an das berühmte Geschmeideviertel des Jewellery Quarter sowie an die industriellen Ursprünge der Stadt erinnern. In ihrem Inneren bildet eine gestaffelte, vom Shakespeare Memorial Room bekrönte Rotunde den Kern einer Anlage aus acht kreisrunden Räumen. Neben drei größeren Lesesälen, einer Kinderbibliothek, Galerien und Cafés verfügt die Bibliothek auch über einen Dachgarten und ein versenktes äußeres Amphitheater. Das von den Architekten auch als „Volkspalast" bezeichnete Gebäude wurde eigens entworfen, um jährlich drei Millionen Besuchern Platz bieten zu können.

Library of Birmingham

Birmingham, England
Mecanoo, 2013

La biblioteca más grande de Europa domina la plaza Centenary Square, en el corazón de Birmingham. Su fachada de cristal, oro y plata está cubierta de miles de anillos metálicos que representan el famoso barrio de la joyería y los orígenes industriales de la ciudad. Por dentro, una rotonda escalonada, coronada por la sala Shakespeare Memorial Room, constituye el eje de ocho espacios circulares. La biblioteca, además de disponer de tres salas de lectura principales, una biblioteca para niños, galerías y cafés, cuenta con un jardín en la azotea y un anfiteatro a cielo abierto, incrustado en el subsuelo. El edificio, definido por su arquitecto como un "palacio del pueblo", ha sido diseñado para un acoger, según las expectativas, a 3 millones de visitantes al año.

La plus vaste bibliothèque d'Europe surplombe Centenary Square en plein centre de Birmingham. D'or, d'argent et de verre, sa façade, habillée de milliers d'anneaux de maille métalliques, rappelle le célèbre quartier des Joailliers de la ville et ses origines industrielles. A l'intérieur, une rotonde étagée, que vient couronner la Salle commémorative Shakespeare (Shakespeare Memorial Room), s'inscrit au cœur de huit espaces circulaires. Outre les trois salles de lecture principales, une bibliothèque pour enfants et plusieurs cafés, le visiteur peut profiter du jardin aménagé sur le toit, ainsi que d'un amphithéâtre encaissé à l'extérieur. Décrite par ses architectes comme un « palais du peuple », la bibliothèque a été conçue pour recevoir les quelques 3 millions de visiteurs escomptés tous les ans.

The British Library became its own
entity in 1973, having previously
been part of the British Museum.
It took twenty-five years, however,
to establish its permanent home at
St Pancras. The architect envisioned
a 'magic mountain of all the knowledge
in the world', and that sense of scale
reverberates inside and out. The
library holds over 150 million items,
including 14 million books, and as
a legal deposit library it adds some
3 million items annually. At the
building's core is the King's Library,
a six-storey glass tower housing
65,000 volumes collected by George
III, and outside, on the piazza, stand
sculptures by Eduardo Paolozzi and
Antony Gormley.

Die Nationalbibliothek des Vereinigten
Königreiches wurde im Jahr 1973 aus
dem Britischen Museum ausgegliedert,
dem sie bis dahin angehörte, und
wird seitdem eigenständig geführt.
Nichtsdestotrotz vergingen 25 Jahre,
bevor sie in St. Pancras ihr ständiges
Zuhause fand. Dem Architekten
schwebte ein „Zauberberg des
Weltwissens" vor und dieser Anspruch
ist innen wie außen deutlich spürbar.
Der Bibliotheksbestand umfasst mehr
als 150 Millionen Artikel, darunter
14 Millionen Bücher, und infolge ihres
Status als Pflichtexemplarbibliothek
kommen jährlich um die drei
Millionen Artikel hinzu. Im Kern des
Gebäudes liegt die King's Library, ein
sechsstöckiger Glasturm, der 65.000
von Georg III. gesammelte Artikel
beherbergt, während auf der Piazza
im Freien Skulpturen von Eduardo
Paolozzi und Antony Gormley stehen.

British Library

London, England
Colin St John Wilson, 1998

La British Library a acquis son statut d'entité distincte en 1973, après avoir dépendu du British Museum. Il a fallu cependant attendre vingt-cinq ans avant qu'elle ne s'établisse de manière permanente à St-Pancras. Conçue par son architecte comme un véritable 'mont prodigieux de tous les savoirs du monde', la bibliothèque laisse transparaître cette idée à l'intérieur comme à l'extérieur. Son fonds réunit plus de 150 millions pièces, dont 14 millions livres, auxquelles s'ajoutent quelques 3 millions d'éléments par an dans le dépôt légal. Le bâtiment abrite en son cœur la King's Library (bibliothèque du Roi), une tour de verre de six étages qui héberge 65 000 volumes réunis par George III. Dans la cour extérieure trônent des sculptures d'Eduardo Paolozzi et d'Antony Gormley.

La Biblioteca Británica se convirtió en entidad propia en 1973, ya que anteriormente formada parte del Museo Británico. Tardó veinticinco años, no obstante, en establecerse en su sede permanente en el barrio de St Pancras. El arquitecto imaginó una «montaña mágica de todos los conocimientos del mundo»·y esta sensación de envergadura resuena dentro y fuera del edificio. La biblioteca contiene más de 150 millones de elementos, incluidos 14 millones de libros; además, como biblioteca de depósito legal, añade unos tres millones de elementos anuales. El alma del edificio lo constituye la Biblioteca del Rey, una torre de cristal de seis plantas que aloja 65.000 volúmenes coleccionados por Jorge III. En el exterior, la plaza está adornada con esculturas de Eduardo Paolozzi y Antony Gormley.

Peckham Library and Media Centre

London, England
Alsop Architects, 2000

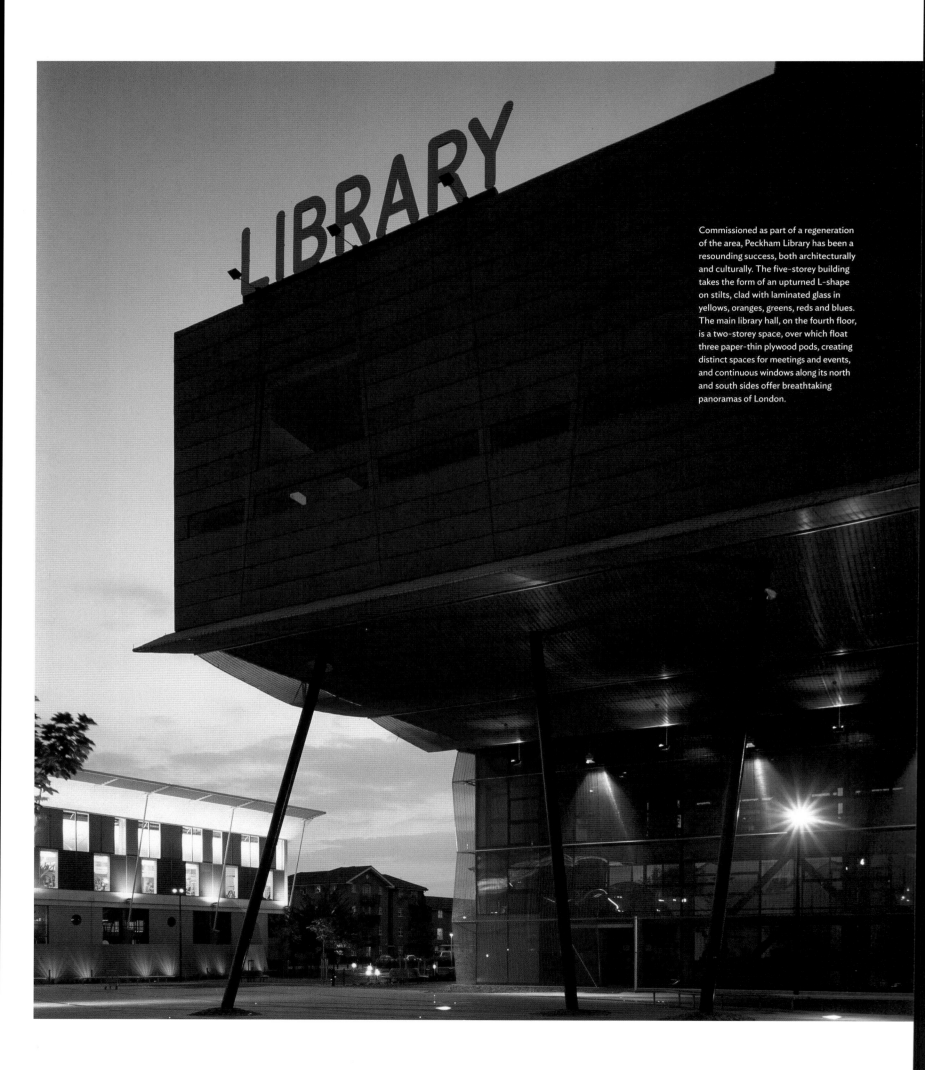

Commissioned as part of a regeneration of the area, Peckham Library has been a resounding success, both architecturally and culturally. The five-storey building takes the form of an upturned L-shape on stilts, clad with laminated glass in yellows, oranges, greens, reds and blues. The main library hall, on the fourth floor, is a two-storey space, over which float three paper-thin plywood pods, creating distinct spaces for meetings and events, and continuous windows along its north and south sides offer breathtaking panoramas of London.

Die als Teil einer Wiederbelebungs-
maßnahme des Stadtteils in Auftrag
gegebene Peckham Library war sowohl
architektonisch als auch kulturell
ein durchschlagender Erfolg. Das
auf Pfeilern ruhende, fünfstöckige
Gebäude in der Form eines aufgestell-
ten L kleidet sich in eine Fassade aus
gelben, orangen, grünen, roten und
blauen Verbundglaselementen. Den im
vierten Stock gelegenen Hauptsaal der
Bibliothek bildet ein zweigeschossiger
Raum, über dem drei hauchdünne
Sperrholzobjekte schweben, wodurch
differenzierte Bereiche für Versamm-
lungen und Veranstaltungen entstehen.
Zudem erlauben Fensterfluchten
sowohl an der Nord- als auch der
Südseite atemberaubende Aussichten auf die Londoner Innenstadt.

Encargada con el objetivo de contribuir
a la regeneración de la zona, la
Biblioteca Peckham ha logrado un
éxito rotundo, tanto desde el punto
de vista arquitectónico como cultural.
El edificio de cinco plantas tiene forma
de una L invertida sobre columnas
y está recubierto de vidrio laminado
en tonos amarillos, naranjas, verdes,
rojos y azules. La sala de la biblioteca
principal, en la cuarta planta, es un
espacio de dos pisos, sobre el que
flotan tres estancias de contrachapado
muy fino, destinadas a reuniones
y eventos diversos. Unas ventanas
continuas a lo largo de sus lados
septentrional y meridional ofrecen
unas vistas impresionantes de Londres.

Commandée dans le cadre d'un
projet de revitalisation du quartier,
la Bibliothèque Peckham a remporté
un énorme succès, tant sur le plan
architectural que culturel. L'édifice
de cinq étages prend la forme d'un
L renversé sur pilotis, habillé de
verres polychromes teintés de jaune,
d'orange, de vert, de rouge et de bleu.
Le hall principal de la bibliothèque,
au quatrième étage, s'organise sur
deux niveaux, surplombés de trois
espèces de cosses en contreplaqué
aussi fin que de papier, qui aménagent
des espaces distincts pour les
rencontres et les événements,
alors que la baie vitrée longeant les
côtés nord et sud offre un aperçu
époustouflant de Londres.

Peckham Library and Media Centre, London, England

Sainte-Geneviève Library

Paris, France
Henri Labrouste, 1851

This library, which inherited the prized collections of the sixth-century Abbey de Sainte-Geneviève, was erected by Henri Labrouste in the Panthéon district between 1844 and 1851. The two-storey façade bears the names of 810 great figures, while inside, the jewel in its crown is the vast reading room that spans the entire upper storey, divided in two by a line of elegant cast-iron Ionic columns. Labrouste's use of iron, highly innovative in his day, made it possible for him to do without the usual cumbersome masonry. Though renovations were carried out in the 1930s and 1960s, the edifice continues to offer both a rational and poetic reflection of the industrial era.

Die von Henri Labrouste zwischen
1844 und 1851 am Place du
Panthéon in Paris erbaute Bibliothek
beherbergt die Sammlung der im
sechsten Jahrhundert begründeten
Abtei Sainte-Geneviève. In ihre
zweistöckige Fassade sind die Namen
von 810 berühmten Persönlichkeiten
eingraviert und das Glanzstück
der Anlage bildet der weitläufige
Leseraum im Gebäudeinneren, der
das gesamte Obergeschoß einnimmt
und von eleganten, ionischen Säulen
aus Gusseisen in zwei Hälften geteilt
wird. Labroustes äußerst innovative
Verwendung von Eisen erlaubte es
ihm, weitestgehend auf schwerfälliges
Mauerwerk zu verzichten. Trotz
zahlreicher Renovierungsarbeiten
kündet das Gebäude unverändert vom
rationalen sowie vom poetischen Glanz
des Industriezeitalters.

Edifiée par Henri Labrouste, place
du Panthéon à Paris, entre 1844 et
1851, cette bibliothèque a hérité de
la précieuse collection de l'Abbaye
Sainte-Geneviève fondée au VIe
siècle. La façade à deux niveaux
porte les noms graves de 810
personnages célèbres, alors que la
vaste salle de lecture, pièce maîtresse
de l'édifice, occupe intégralement
l'étage supérieur, divisé en deux par
de fines colonnes ioniques en fonte.
Très innovante à l'époque, cette
utilisation apparente du métal par
Labrouste lui a permis de se passer
de lourds ouvrages de maçonnerie.
Malgré plusieurs rénovations, le
bâtiment continue d'offrir une
interprétation à la fois rationnelle et
poétique de l'époque industrielle.

Esta biblioteca parisiense, situada en la plaza del Panteón y construida por Henri Labrouste entre 1844 y 1851, heredó la invaluable colección de la Abadía de Sainte-Geneviève, fundada en el siglo VI. En la fachada de dos pisos están inscritos los nombres de 810 personajes célebres mientras que, en el interior, la joya de la corona es la espaciosa sala de lectura que ocupa toda la planta superior, dividida en dos por elegantes columnas jónicas de hierro fundido. El uso del metal a la vista por parte de Labrouste, que le permitió prescindir de una voluminosa mampostería, fue algo muy innovador en su momento. A pesar de las diversas renovaciones realizadas desde entonces, el edificio sigue representando una interpretación a la vez racional y poética de la era industrial.

Dipòsit de les Aigües Library

Pompeu Fabra University, Barcelona, Spain
Lluís Clotet & Ignacio Paricio Ansuátegui, 1999

When Pompeu Fabra University was established in 1990, it chose to locate its campus in the heart of Barcelona, between the old town and the district built for the 1992 Olympic Games. Its main library is formed by the Jaume I building and the Dipòsit de les Aigües Library, which are connected by an underpass. The latter, with its atmospheric reading room, houses the university's special collections, but it began life as a reservoir for the nearby Parc de la Ciutadella. Modelled on a Roman prototype, it was designed in 1874 by Josep Fontserè, with some assistance from a then-unknown architecture student, Antoni Gaudí.

Bei ihrer Gründung im Jahr 1990 wurde entschieden, den Campus der Universität Pompeu Fabra im Herzen Barcelonas anzusiedeln, zwischen der Altstadt und dem für die Olympischen Spiele 1992 errichteten Stadtteil. Die Hauptbibliothek besteht aus einem, Jakob I. dem Eroberer gewidmeten Gebäude sowie dem Dipòsit de les Aigües, die durch eine Unterführung miteinander verbunden sind. Das ursprünglich als Wasserspeicher für den nahegelegenen Parc de la Ciutadella genutzte Dipòsit verfügt über einen stimmungsvollen Leseraum und beherbergt heute die Sonderbestände der Universität. Entworfen wurde es im Jahr 1874 von Josep Fontserè, der sich an einem römischen Modell inspirierte, und sich dabei von einem damals noch völlig unbekannten Architekturstudenten namens Antoni Gaudí zur Hand gehen ließ.

Lorsque l'Université Pompeu Fabra fut établie en 1990, il a été décidé d'implanter son campus en plein centre de Barcelone, à mi-chemin entre le cœur historique de la ville et le nouveau quartier construit pour les Jeux Olympiques de 1992. Sa principale bibliothèque se répartit entre le bâtiment Jaume I et le Dipòsit de les Aigües, reliés entre eux par un passage souterrain. Avec sa salle de lecture propice à l'étude, ce dernier bâtiment abrite désormais les collections spéciales de l'Université, après avoir initialement fait office de bassin annexe au Parc de la Citadelle, tout proche. S'inspirant des modèles de l'architecture romaine, Josep Fontserè conçut ce parc en 1874 avec l'aide d'un étudiant en architecture alors inconnu, Antoni Gaudi.

Cuando se fundó la Universidad Pompeu Fabra en 1990, se decidió establecer su campus en el centro de Barcelona, entre el casco antiguo y el barrio olímpico, construido para las Olimpiadas de 1992. Su principal biblioteca está constituida por el edificio Jaume I y el Dipòsit de les Aigües, conectados entre sí por un paso subterráneo. El segundo, con su evocadora sala de lectura, alberga las colecciones especiales de la universidad pero, en su día, fue un depósito de agua para el cercano Parc de la Ciutadella. Inspirado en un prototipo romano, fue diseñado en 1874 por Josep Fontserè, que contó con la ayuda del estudiante de arquitectura, por entonces desconocido, Antoni Gaudí.

Located in Spijkenisse's market square, within a new eco-housing development, 'Book Mountain' is a monument to reading. Beneath the glass and timber pyramid shell, a core of closed spaces is surrounded by five storeys of book stacks. Balconies and stairs run around the pyramid's sides, culminating at the apex in a reading room and café with a 360° view of the area. In the face of growing digitisation, the library invites readers to explore and interact with the books, and the space they inhabit, and at night it is an illuminated beacon for the town.

Der am Marktplatz von Spijkenisse innerhalb einer ökologischen Wohnsiedlung errichtete Bücherberg ist ein Denkmal zu Ehren des Lesens. Im Inneren der aus Glas und Holz errichteten Außenpyramide liegt ein Bereich aus abgetrennten Räumen, den fünf Geschosse mit Bücherregalen einrahmen. Balkone und Treppen führen über die Pyramidenseiten zum Leseraum bzw. Kaffeehaus in der Pyramidenspitze, die einen Rundblick über die umliegende Stadt bietet. Angesichts der fortschreitenden Digitalisierung lädt diese Bibliothek ihre Besucher dazu ein, Bücher und den von ihnen beanspruchten Raum zu erforschen und damit zu interagieren. Nachts verwandelt sich die Bibliothek außerdem in einen innerstädtischen Leuchtturm.

Book Mountain

Spijkenisse, The Netherlands
MVRDV, 2012

Située sur la place du marché de Spijkenisse, dans un nouveau complexe d'éco-habitats, la 'Book Mountain' est un monument tout entier dédié à la lecture. Sous l'enveloppe pyramidale faite de verre et de bois se dresse un cocon d'espaces clos encerclé d'étagères de livres réparties sur cinq niveaux. Des balcons et des escaliers courent tout le long de l'édifice, de chaque côté de la pyramide, et mènent, en son sommet, à une salle de lecture et un café offrant une vue panoramique de la région. Face à la digitalisation grandissante, la bibliothèque invite le lecteur à explorer et à interagir avec les livres et l'espace qu'ils occupent. La nuit venue, telle un phare, la bibliothèque illumine la ville.

Situada en la plaza del mercado de Spijkenisse, con una nueva evolución de la envoltura ecológica, la «Montaña de Libros» representa un monumento a la lectura. Bajo la estructura piramidal de cristal y madera, un núcleo de espacios cerrados está rodeado de cinco plantas de estanterías de libros. Unas galerías y escaleras recorren los laterales de la pirámide y culminan en el vértice con una sala de lectura y un café que proporcionan unas vistas de 360 grados de la zona. Frente a la creciente digitalización, la biblioteca invita a los lectores a explorar y a interactuar con los libros y el espacio que habitan. De noche, se alza como un faro luminoso para la ciudad.

TU Delft Library

Delft, The Netherlands
Mecanoo, 1997

When designing the library to sit opposite TUD's brutalistic auditorium, Mecanoo decided not to complement it in a traditional sense, but to create a sloped plane, which inserts the library into the landscape and creates the sense that the former is floating. The library's roof is covered with grass, which serves as natural insulation and additional public space, but its most distinguishing feature is the steel cone that appears to pin down the grass roof. A spiral staircase within this leads to four storeys of reading rooms, and on two lower levels, the stacks are suspended along one electric-blue wall.

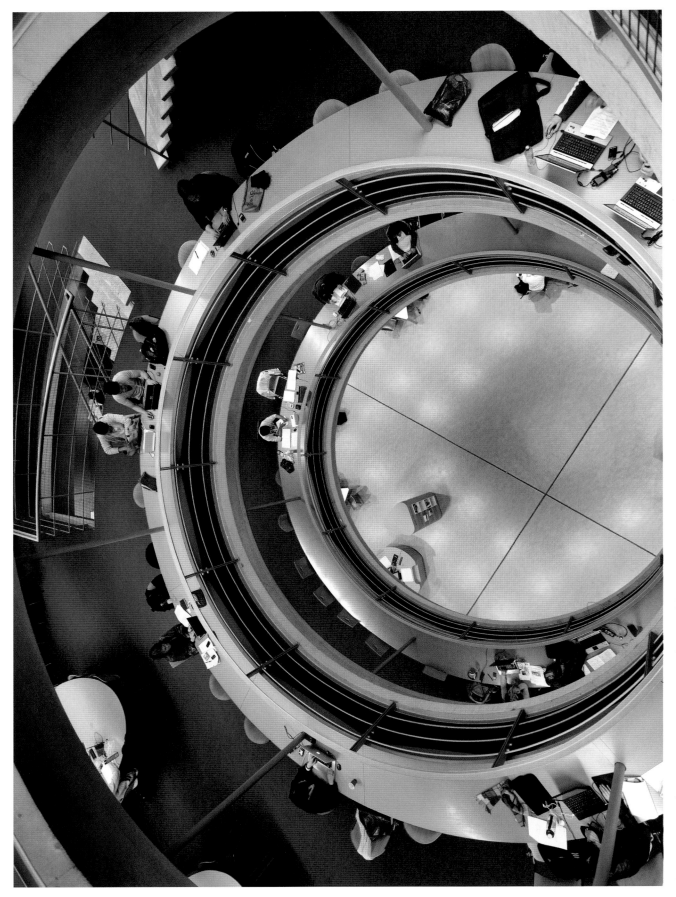

Bei ihrem Entwurf für die gegenüber des brutalistischen Hörsaals der TU Delft geplanten Bibliothek entschlossen sich Mecanoo dazu, diesen nicht auf die herkömmliche Art und Weise zu ergänzen, sondern eine geneigte Ebene zu schaffen, um die Bibliothek derart in die Landschaft einzufügen und ihr einen schwebenden Aspekt zu verleihen. Das Dach der Bibliothek wurde mit Gras gedeckt, was einerseits als natürliche Isolierung dient und andererseits einen zusätzlichen öffentlichen Raum schafft. Ihr charakteristischstes Merkmal bildet jedoch zweifelsfrei jener Stahlkegel, der das Grasdach aufzuspießen scheint. Im Kegelinneren führt eine Wendeltreppe zu den auf vier Stockwerken gelegenen Leseräumen und auf zwei unteren Ebenen finden sich entlang einer grellblauen Wand hängende Bücherregale.

Au moment de concevoir la bibliothèque qui devait faire face au style brutaliste de l'auditorium de la TUD, Mecanoo abandonna l'idée de tout prolongement au sens conventionnel du terme pour créer un plan incliné qui insère naturellement la bibliothèque dans le paysage et donne l'impression d'un bâtiment en apesanteur. La toiture de la bibliothèque, recouverte d'herbe, fait office d'isolant naturel tout en aménageant un espace public supplémentaire. Cependant, l'ouvrage frappe surtout par le cône en acier qui semble épingler le toit d'herbe. A l'intérieur, un escalier en spirale distribue l'espace entre quatre niveaux de salles de lecture et deux autres niveaux inférieurs où les étagères sont suspendues le long d'un mur bleu électrique.

Al diseñar esta biblioteca frente al auditorio brutalista del TUD, Mecanoo decidió no ejecutarla en un sentido tradicional sino crear un plano inclinado que insertara la biblioteca en el paisaje y diera la sensación de que estaba flotando. El tejado de la biblioteca está cubierto de hierba, que sirve de aislante natural y ofrece un espacio público adicional, pero su característica más distintiva es el cono de acero que parece clavarse en el tejado de hierba. Una escalera en espiral en su interior conduce a cuatro plantas de salas de lectura y a dos niveles inferiores. Las estanterías están suspendidas a lo largo de una pared de color azul eléctrico.

John a Lasco Library

Emden, Germany

Jochen Bunse, 1995

In the mid-sixteenth century, Emden was an important centre for the Protestant Reformation, under the pastorship of Polish nobleman John a Lasco. In 1943, its late-Gothic Great church, the mother church of the Calvinists of north-west of Germany, was severely damaged by bombs, leaving only the outer walls and arcades. The ruin remained untouched until the early 1990s, when it was decided to incorporate it into a new library building. The library has approximately 3,000 square metres of actual space and 13,000 cubic metres of renovated space, and the modern architecture contrasts openly and harmoniously with the historical ruins.

Mitte des 16. Jahrhunderts war Emden unter dem Pastor und polnischen Adeligen Johannes a Lasco ein bedeutendes Zentrum der protestantischen Reformation. 1943 wurde die von den Calvinisten Nordwestdeutschlands als Mutterkirche verehrte spätgotische Große Kirche der Stadt durch Bombentreffer so schwer beschädigt, dass danach nur noch die Außenmauern und Arkaden standen. Die Ruine blieb bis in die frühen 1990er-Jahre unangetastet, bis schließlich der Beschluss gefasst wurde, diese in ein neues Bibliotheksgebäude zu integrieren. Die Bibliothek verfügt über eine Nutzfläche von ungefähr 3000 m² sowie ein renoviertes Raumvolumen von 13.000 m³ und die moderne Bauweise kontrastiert offen und harmonisch mit den geschichtsträchtigen Überresten.

John a Lasco Library, Emden, Germany

Au milieu du seizième siècle, Emden était un important lieu de la Réforme protestante, sous le pastorat de Jean de Lasco, réformateur polonais d'origine noble. En 1943, les bombardements ont quasiment détruit la Grande Eglise d'Emden, mère de l'église des calvinistes du Nord-Ouest de l'Allemagne, construite dans le style du gothique tardif, dont il ne restait que les murs extérieurs et les arcades. Les ruines sont demeurées en l'état jusqu'au début des années 90, après qu'il ait été décidé de les intégrer dans une nouvelle bibliothèque. Le bâtiment s'étend sur près de 3 000 mètres carrés et intègre 13 000 mètres cubes d'espace restauré. Le contraste entre l'architecture moderne et les ruines historiques traduit un parti pris audacieux mais non moins harmonieux.

A mediados del siglo XVI, Emden constituía un centro importante de la Reforma Protestante, bajo el mandato pastoral del noble polaco Johannes a Lasco. En 1943, su gran iglesia gótica tardía, la madre iglesia de los calvinistas del noroeste de Alemania, fue gravemente dañada por las bombas que dejaron en pie solo los muros y las arcadas. Las ruinas siguieron intactas hasta principios de la década de 1990 cuando se decidió incorporarlas al nuevo edificio de la biblioteca. La biblioteca ofrece aproximadamente 3.000 metros cuadrados de espacio real y 13.000 metros cúbicos de espacio renovado. La arquitectura moderna contrasta abierta y armoniosamente con las ruinas históricas.

Vennesla Library and Culture House

Vennesla, Norway
Helen & Hard, 2011

In 2005, the Municipality of Vennesla decided to relocate its library to the city centre, linking it with existing community and educational facilities to create a cultural hub. The new library's most distinguishing feature is its ceiling, comprised of twenty-seven prefabricated glued-laminated timber ribs. The ribs gradually shift throughout the interior to inform the library's different spaces and the geometry of the roof, before joining with the ground floor as furniture, accommodating stacks and seating. The distinctive 'whale-skeleton' structure and generous use of glass make this a bright, striking library that has become part of the urban fabric.

Im Jahr 2005 beschloss die Kommune Vennesla, ihre Bibliothek in die Innenstadt zu verlegen und sie dort mit bereits bestehenden kommunalen bzw. Bildungseinrichtungen zu einem Kulturzentrum zu verbinden. Das einprägsamste Merkmal der neuen Bibliothek ist wohl ihre Decke aus 27 vorgefertigten Rippen aus Brettschichtholz. Diese Rippen durchziehen das gesamte Gebäude und prägen sämtliche Innenräume sowie die Geometrie des Daches, bevor sie sich im Erdgeschoß in Mobiliar verwandeln und als solches Bücherregale beherbergen bzw. Sitzgelegenheiten bilden. Dank diesem unverkennbaren „Walgerippe" sowie der großzügigen Verwendung von Glas bildet diese helle und markante Bibliothek einen harmonischen Bestandteil des städtischen Gefüges.

En 2005, la municipalité de Vennesla a décidé de relocaliser sa bibliothèque au centre-ville, en la reliant aux espaces communautaires et éducatifs déjà en place pour aménager un vaste carrefour culturel. La nouvelle bibliothèque surprend par son plafond, composé de vingt-sept arrêtes préfabriquées en bois lamellé-collé, qui délimitent progressivement sur toute la longueur intérieure des espaces distincts et structurent la géométrie du toit, avant de se rejoindre au rez-de-chaussée sous forme de mobilier intégré aménageant des étagères et des sièges. La structure atypique rappelant l'ossature d'une baleine et l'usage généreux de verre font de cet édifice une bibliothèque lumineuse et surprenante devenue indissociable du paysage urbain.

En 2005, el municipio de Vennesla decidió trasladar su biblioteca al centro de la ciudad, vinculándola con las infraestructuras educativas y comunitarias existentes a fin de crear un núcleo cultural. La característica más distintiva de la nueva biblioteca es su techo, que consta de veintisiete costillas de madera prefabricadas laminadas y encoladas. Las costillas cambian gradualmente en el interior para conformar los distintos espacios de la biblioteca y la geometría del tejado, antes de unirse con la planta baja en forma de mueble, donde se alojan estanterías y asientos. La singular estructura de «esqueleto de ballena» y el uso generoso del cristal la convierten en una biblioteca luminosa y llamativa que ha pasado a formar parte del tejido urbano.

Library of the Faculty of Law

University of Zurich, Switzerland
Santiago Calatrava, 2004

When designing a new library for the courtyard of Fietz's 1909 building, which previously housed the chemistry department, respect for the original building was paramount. Inspired by libraries of the Renaissance and Baroque periods, Calatrava inserted the library like a piece of furniture, barely impacting the exterior. Upon entering, one's eyes are immediately drawn upwards to the bright timber galleries, which surround an asymmetric elliptic atrium, reaching from the first floor to the seventh. It is roofed with a glass cupola which tempers the heat and light throughout the seasons. The books are clearly displayed, while the library appears to hover over the courtyard.

Der Entwurf für eine neue Bibliothek im Innenhof des von Hermann Fietz im Jahre 1909 errichteten Gebäudes, in dem sich zuvor das Institut für Chemie befunden hatte, sollte möglichst von Eingriffen in die ursprüngliche Struktur absehen. Calatrava inspirierte sich an Bibliotheken der Renaissance und des Barock und fügte seine Konstruktion, einem Möbelstück gleich, in die bestehende Substanz ein, ohne dabei das Exterieur übermäßig zu verändern. Beim Betreten des Gebäudes wandern die Blicke wie magisch angezogen zu den hellen Holzgalerien empor, die den siebenstöckigen Rahmen des asymmetrisch elliptischen Atriums bilden. Eine gläserne Kuppel dämpft das im Jahreslauf einfallende Licht und die Hitze. Die Bücher sind gut sichtbar präsentiert und die Bibliothek scheint gleichsam über dem Innenhof zu schweben.

La conception d'une nouvelle bibliothèque dans le bâtiment de la cour de Fietz, de 1909, qui abritait précédemment la faculté de chimie, se devait à tout prix de respecter la structure initiale. Inspiré par les bibliothèques des époques Renaissance et Baroque, Calatrava a conçu son ouvrage comme une pièce du mobilier existant, sans incidences ou presque sur l'extérieur. Dès l'entrée, le regard du visiteur est immédiatement attiré vers le haut par les galeries en bois clair encerclant un atrium en forme d'ellipse asymétrique, qui s'élève du premier au septième niveau. L'édifice est recouvert d'une cupule vitrée qui tempère la chaleur et tamise la lumière au gré des saisons. Les livres sont clairement exposés, alors que la bibliothèque semble planer au-dessus de la cour.

Al diseñar una nueva biblioteca para el patio del edificio de 1909 de Fietz, en el que anteriormente se encontraba el departamento de química, el respeto por el edificio original era una cuestión fundamental. Inspirándose en las bibliotecas renacentistas y barrocas, Calatrava la insertó como si de un mueble se tratara, lo que apenas supuso un impacto para el exterior. Tras entrar en ella, la mirada se dirige de inmediato hacia arriba a las galerías de madera clara que rodean un atrio elíptico y asimétrico, que llega desde el primer piso hasta el séptimo. Está techada con una cúpula acristalada que atenúa el calor y la luz a lo largo de las estaciones. Los libros están claramente expuestos, mientras que la biblioteca parece planear sobre el patio.

In 2011, the Stuttgart City Library (founded in 1901) relocated its central operation to the up-and-coming district of Mailänder Platz. The new nine-storey library has a double façade; an austere exterior of grey concrete and frosted glass, and an inner shell of glass, surrounding a bright and spacious heart. Here, books and readers provide the colour, and a central roof light is reflected in a ground-floor fountain, asserting the library as a meditative space. A minimalist Pantheon, it is an introverted and democratic place that shows due reverence to the physical book.

Im Jahr 2011 bezog die Zentralbibliothek der exakt 110 Jahre zuvor gegründeten Stadtbibliothek Stuttgart ihr neues Zuhause im aufstrebenden Stadtteil am Mailänder Platz. Das neue neunstöckige Gebäude verfügt über eine Doppelfassade, ein strenges Exterieur aus grauem Beton und mattiertem Glas sowie eine gläserne Innenschale, die das helle und weitläufige Herzstück des Gebäudes umschließt. Hier sorgen vor allem die aufbewahrten Bücher und ihre Leser für Farbakzente und eine zentrale Deckenleuchte, die sich in einem Brunnen im Erdgeschoß spiegelt, verstärkt das meditative Ambiente der Bibliothek noch weiter. Dieses minimalistische Pantheon ist gleichsam ein introvertierter und demokratischer Ort, der dem materiellen Buch die gebührende Ehre erweist.

En 2011, La bibliothèque municipale de Stuttgart (fondée en 1901) a relocalisé son centre opérationnel dans le nouveau quartier de Mailänder Platz. La nouvelle bibliothèque construite sur neuf étages se distingue par une double façade ; un cadre extérieur austère en béton gris dans lequel viennent s'encastrer des verres dépolis dissimule une enveloppe intérieure vitrée, qui encercle un cœur lumineux et spacieux. Ici, les livres et les lecteurs apportent des touches de couleur, alors que la lumière centrale émise par la verrière zénithale se reflète dans une fontaine au rez-de-chaussée, dégageant une atmosphère propice à la méditation. A l'instar d'un panthéon minimaliste, la bibliothèque offre un lieu introverti et démocratique bâti à la gloire du Livre.

En 2011, la Biblioteca Municipal de Stuttgart (fundada en 1901) trasladó su sede central al vecino barrio de Mailänder Platz. La nueva biblioteca de nueve plantas presenta una doble fachada, un exterior austero de hormigón gris y cristal esmerilado, y una estructura interior acristalada, que rodea un centro luminoso y espacioso. Aquí, los libros y los lectores son los que proporcionan el colorido, y una claraboya central se refleja en la fuente de la planta baja, lo que reafirma la biblioteca como espacio de meditación. Cual panteón minimalista, constituye un lugar introvertido y democrático que muestra el debido respeto al libro físico.

Stuttgart City Library

Stuttgart, Germany
Yi Architects, 2011

Abbey Library of St Gall

St Gallen, Switzerland
Peter Thumb, 1767

Founded in 719 by St Othmar, the abbey can trace its origins to a hermitage set up by the Irish monk Gall in the previous century. After the disruption of the Reformation, the monastery's own craftsmen remodelled the abbey in the Baroque style, but in 1798 it was attacked by French soldiers and the monks fled, taking with them the library's precious collection. The monastery was dissolved in 1805, but it was decided to preserve the library. Its interior is a rich mix of wood, stucco, and frescoes depicting scenes befitting this 'Sanatorium of the Soul'. The abbey became a UNESCO World Heritage site in 1983.

Fondée en 719 par Saint Othmar, l'abbaye tire son origine de l'ermitage établi par le moine irlandais Gall, le siècle précédent. Après les perturbations de la Réforme, les artisans du monastère entreprirent eux-mêmes de refaçonner l'abbaye dans le style baroque. Attaqués par l'armée française en 1798, les moines s'enfuirent emportant avec eux la précieuse collection de la bibliothèque. Le monastère fut détruit en 1805. Il fut cependant décidé d'en préserver la bibliothèque, dont l'intérieur est somptueusement décoré de boiseries, de stuc et de fresques représentant d'humbles scènes adaptées de ce 'Sanatorium de l'âme'. L'abbaye a été inscrite au patrimoine mondial en 1983.

Die im Jahr 719 vom heiligen Otmar gegründete Fürstabtei kann ihren Ursprung auf die ein Jahrhundert zuvor vom irischen Mönch Gall an dieser Stelle errichtete Klause zurückführen. Nach den Zerrüttungen der Reformation wurde die Abtei von den Klosterhandwerkern selbst im Barockstil umgestaltet, im Jahr 1798 wurde sie jedoch von französischen Truppen angegriffen, woraufhin die Mönche mitsamt der kostbaren Bibliothekssammlung die Flucht ergriffen. Zwar wurde das Kloster 1805 aufgelassen, jedoch wurde gleichzeitig beschlossen, die Bibliothek zu erhalten. Ihr Interieur verbindet Holz, Stuck und Fresken zu einem prächtigen Ganzen und zeigt Abbildungen, deren Bescheidenheit diesem „Sanatorium der Seele" zur Ehre gereicht. Im Jahr 1983 wurde der Abtei schließlich der Titel einer Weltkulturerbestätte verliehen.

Fundada en 719 por San Otmaro, la abadía puede remontar sus orígenes a una ermita construida por el monje irlandés Galo en el siglo anterior. Tras la interrupción de la Reforma, los propios artesanos del monasterio remodelaron la abadía en estilo barroco pero en 1798 fue atacado por soldados franceses, lo que provocó la huida de los monjes que se llevaron con ellos la valiosa colección de la biblioteca. El monasterio se disolvió en 1805 pero se decidió conservar la biblioteca. Su interior presenta una espléndida combinación de madera, estucos y frescos que representan unas sencillas escenas apropiadas para este «Sanatorio del alma». La abadía fue declarada Patrimonio de la Humanidad en 1983.

Laurentian Library

Florence, Italy
Michelangelo Buonarroti, 1571

The Laurentian Library was commissioned by Pope Clement VII to
convey the ascent of his family, the
Medicis, to the ranks of the elite.
Situated in the Basilica of St Lawrence,
it was designed by Michelangelo in
1523. After 1534, when Michelangelo
left Florence, the work was taken over,
using the architect's plans, by Tribolo,
Vasari, and Ammannati. It was finally
completed almost fifty years later.
Because of its revolutionary use of
space – particularly in the vestibule,
with its complex staircase – it is
considered Michelangelo's greatest
architectural work, and it is roundly
regarded as a prototype of mannerism.

Die kurz Laurenziana genannte
Bibliothek wurde von Papst Clemens
VII. in Auftrag gegeben, um den
Aufstieg seiner Familie, der Medici, in
den Kreis der Elite zu unterstreichen.
Die in der Basilica di San Lorenzo
gelegene Bibliothek wurde im Jahr
1523 von Michelangelo entworfen
und nachdem dieser Florenz im
Jahr 1534 verlassen hatte von
Tribolo, Vasari und Ammannati
nach den Originalentwürfen des
Universalgenies fortgeführt. Die
Fertigstellung erfolgte jedoch erst
knapp 50 Jahre später. Aufgrund
der revolutionären Raumnutzung –
insbesondere im Vestibül mit seinem
komplexen Treppenaufgang – gilt
die Bibliothek als Michelangelos
größtes Meisterwerk und einhellig
als Prototyp des Manierismus.

La Bibliothèque Laurentienne fut commandée par le Pape Clément VII, désireux d'ériger l'ascension de sa famille, les Médicis, au rang d'élite. Située dans l'enceinte du monastère San Lorenzo, la bibliothèque a été conçue par Michel-Ange en 1523. En 1534, lorsque Michel-Ange quitta Florence, les travaux furent respectivement poursuivis, selon les plans de l'architecte, par Tribolo, Vasari, et Ammannati, pour finalement s'achever près de cinquante ans plus tard. En raison de l'utilisation révolutionnaire de l'espace, notamment dans le vestibule, avec son escalier complexe, l'édifice est considéré comme le chef-d'œuvre architectural de Michel-Ange, jugé carrément précurseur du maniérisme.

La Biblioteca Laurenciana fue encargada por el papa Clemente VII para reflejar el ascenso de su familia, los Médicis, al rango de la élite. Situada en la basílica de San Lorenzo, fue diseñada por Miguel Ángel en 1523. Ya en 1534, cuando Miguel Ángel dejó Florencia, las obras prosiguieron, siguiendo los planos del arquitecto, bajo el mando de Tribolo, Vasari y Ammannati. Finalmente, se completó después de casi cincuenta años. Debido a su revolucionario uso del espacio, en particular, en el vestíbulo con su compleja escalera, está considerada como la obra arquitectónica más importante de Miguel Ángel y como un rotundo prototipo del manierismo.

Duchess Anna Amalia Library

Weimar, Germany
Unknown, restoration by Walther Grunwald, 1776

L'origine de cette bibliothèque remonte à 1552, bien que son emplacement actuel, dans le Grünen Schloss (petit château vert) du seizième siècle, date de 1766. Les niveaux supérieurs de la bibliothèque furent entièrement détruits en 2004 par un incendie dévastateur. Restauré, l'édifice a rouvert ses portes en 2007. Aujourd'hui, la collection comprend près d'un million de volumes. Spécialement aménagée sous le toit, la salle de lecture, avec son décor fonctionnel, offre un contraste saisissant avec le célèbre hall d'inspiration rococo. La bibliothèque a été inscrite au patrimoine mondial de l'UNESCO en 1998.

La historia de esta biblioteca se remonta al año 1552, aunque lleva en su emplazamiento actual, en el castillo Grünen Schloss del siglo XVI, desde 1766. En 2004, se declaró un incendio devastador que destruyó las plantas superiores. El edificio restaurado se volvió a inaugurar en 2007. En la actualidad, la colección abarca alrededor de un millón de volúmenes y se ha creado una sala de lectura especial bajo el tejado, cuya decoración funcional contrasta vivamente con la famosa Sala Rococó. Fue declarada Patrimonio de la Humanidad de la UNESCO en 1998.

The history of this library reaches back as far as 1552, although it has resided at its current site, in the sixteenth-century Grünen Schloss, since 1766. In 2004, a devastating fire broke out and destroyed the upper floors. The restored building was re-inaugurated in 2007. Today, the collection encompasses around 1 million volumes, and a special reading room has been created under the roof, its functional decor in sharp contrast to the famous Rococo Hall. It became a UNESCO World Heritage Site in 1998.

Die altehrwürdige Geschichte dieser Bibliothek reicht bis in das Jahr 1552 zurück. Gleichwohl befindet sie sich erst seit 1766 an ihrem jetzigen Standort im aus dem 16. Jahrhundert stammenden Grünen Schloss. Im Jahr 2004 zerstörte ein verheerender Brand die oberen Geschosse des Gebäudes, das anschließend restauriert und 2007 neu eröffnet wurde. Heute umfasst die Sammlung ungefähr eine Million Exemplare und ein eigener Leseraum, dessen funktionales Dekor in starkem Kontrast zum berühmten Rokokosaal steht, wurde unterhalb des Daches eingerichtet. Seit 1998 gilt die Biblio-thek als UNESCO-Weltkulturerbestätte.

Duchess Anna Amalia Library, Weimar, Germany

Luckenwalde Library

Luckenwalde, Germany
FF Architekten & Martina Wronna, 2008

Luckenwalde's location on the Berlin–Dresden railway line made it a centre of industry in the early twentieth century, so when it received EU URBAN sponsorship in the early twenty-first century, it was decided to convert the heritage-protected railway building into the town library, adding a new annex to house the children's and young people's section. The architects envisioned this annex as an abstract sculpture; its striking exterior almost seems to be pulling away from its traditional neighbour, and the gold shingles of copper-aluminium alloy create a shimmering surface that changes with the light and the weather.

Luckenwaldes Lage an der Bahnstrecke Berlin–Dresden verdankte sich zu Beginn des 20. Jahrhunderts der Aufstieg des Städtchens zu einer Industriehochburg. Als dem Ort hundert Jahre später Fördergelder aus der EU-Gemeinschaftsinitiative URBAN gewährt wurden, fiel die Entscheidung, das denkmalgeschützte Empfangsgebäude des Bahnhofs in eine Stadtbibliothek umzuwandeln und dieses gleichzeitig um einen Anbau für die Kinder- und Jugendbibliothek zu erweitern. Für deren Gestaltung schwebte den Architekten eine abstrakte Skulptur vor und tatsächlich scheint sich das auffällige Äußere von seinem altehrwürdigen Nachbar losreißen zu wollen. Die Goldschindeln des Anbaus aus einer Kupfer-Aluminium-Legierung bilden eine schimmernde Oberfläche, die sich je nach Licht und Wetter anders präsentiert.

El emplazamiento de Luckenwalde en la línea ferroviaria de Berlín a Dresde convirtió a esta localidad en un centro industrial a comienzos del siglo XX por lo que, al recibir el patrocinio EU URBAN a principios del siglo XXI, se decidió transformar el edificio protegido de la estación de ferrocarril en biblioteca municipal y se añadió un nuevo anexo para acoger la sección infantil y juvenil. Los arquitectos concibieron este anexo como una escultura abstracta; su llamativo exterior parece casi estar tirando de su tradicional vecino y las placas doradas de una aleación de cobre y aluminio crean una superficie brillante que cambia con la luz y el tiempo.

Située sur la ligne ferroviaire qui rallie Berlin à Dresde, la ville de Luckenwalde est devenue un véritable centre industriel au début de vingtième siècle. Inscrite au programme URBAN subventionné par l'Union européenne en ce début de vingt-et-unième siècle, la ville a décidé de transformer l'ancienne gare inscrite à son patrimoine en une bibliothèque municipale, en y annexant une extension destinée à la section enfants et jeunes publics. Les architectes ont conçu cette annexe comme une sculpture abstraite, qui frappe par son aspect extérieur semblant presque se détacher de son cadre plus conventionnel. Les écailles dorées en alliage cuivre-aluminium créent une surface chatoyante dont les reflets changent au gré de la luminosité et du temps.

The Black Diamond, Royal Library of Denmark

Copenhagen, Denmark
schmidt hammer lassen architects, 1999

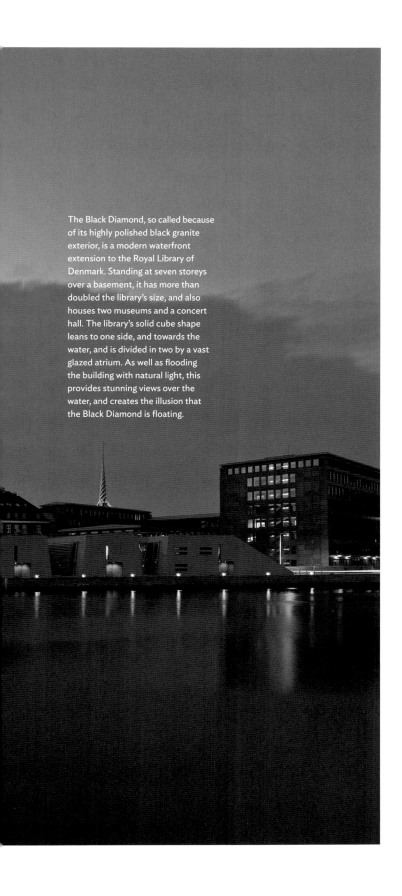

The Black Diamond, so called because of its highly polished black granite exterior, is a modern waterfront extension to the Royal Library of Denmark. Standing at seven storeys over a basement, it has more than doubled the library's size, and also houses two museums and a concert hall. The library's solid cube shape leans to one side, and towards the water, and is divided in two by a vast glazed atrium. As well as flooding the building with natural light, this provides stunning views over the water, and creates the illusion that the Black Diamond is floating.

Dieser moderne und unmittelbar am Wasser gelegene Anbau der Dänischen Königlichen Bibliothek wird aufgrund seiner auf Hochglanz polierten Fassade aus schwarzem Granit auch „Black Diamond" oder "Schwarzer Diamant" genannt. Die aus einem Untergeschoß und sieben Stockwerken bestehende Konstruktion, dank der sich die Bibliotheksfläche mehr als verdoppelt, beherbergt außerdem zwei Museen und einen Konzertsaal. Der massive und zur Wasserseite hin geneigte Kubus wird von einem imposanten verglasten Atrium in zwei Hälften geteilt, wodurch das derart mit Tageslicht durchflutete Gebäude atemberaubende Aussichten auf die umliegenden Wasserflächen gewährt und gleichsam über diesen zu schweben scheint.

Le Diamant noir, ainsi appelé en raison de son enveloppe extérieure en granite noir poli, est une extension moderne, à fleur d'eau, de la Bibliothèque royale du Danemark. Erigé en sept étages au-dessus d'un sous-sol, le bâtiment a plus que doubler le volume de la bibliothèque, et héberge également deux musées et une salle de concert. Oblique d'un côté, le cube formé par la bibliothèque s'avance en direction de l'eau. Il est coupé en deux par un vaste atrium vitré qui inonde l'édifice de lumière naturelle. La vue exceptionnelle qu'il offre sur l'eau donne en outre l'impression d'un Diamant noir en apesanteur.

El Diamante Negro, llamado así por su brillante exterior de granito negro, constituye una moderna ampliación, a orillas del mar, de la Real Biblioteca de Dinamarca. Con siete plantas y un sótano, ha más que duplicado el tamaño de la biblioteca. En ella tienen cabida, igualmente, dos museos y una sala de conciertos. La forma de cubo macizo de la biblioteca se inclina lateralmente hacia el agua. Un amplio atrio de cristal divide el edificio en dos. A la vez que inunda el edificio de luz natural, proporciona unas asombrosas vistas marítimas, dando la impresión de que el Diamante Negro está flotando.

Halmstad City Library

Halmstad, Sweden
schmidt hammer lassen architects, 2006

Set in parkland on the River Nissan,
overlooking the historic city centre,
every element of Halmstad's City Library
has been considered with respect to its
location. Simple materials – concrete,
glass and Nordic larch flooring – form
a bright and open space; the atrium,
linking all three storeys, encircles a

Jedes einzelne Element der in eine Parklandschaft am Ufer des Nissan erbauten und über der Altstadt aufragenden Stadtbibliothek von Halmstad wurde mit Bedacht und unter Berücksichtigung des Standorts gewählt. Schlichte Baumaterialien wie Beton, Glas oder Dielen aus Nordischer Lärche schaffen einen hellen und offenen Raum. Das alle drei Stockwerke verbindende Atrium umrahmt einen statuenhaften Kastanienbaum und die langgezogene, konkave Glasfassade flutet die Bibliothek mit Licht, wodurch sie mit der umliegenden Landschaft zu verschmelzen scheint. Dieses Motiv setzt sich im Außenbereich des Gebäudes fort, wo der Säulenwald die auf ihm ruhende Bibliothek über das Straßenniveau bzw. das vorbeifließende Gewässer hinaus anhebt.

Sur les berges du fleuve Nissan, dans le parc qui surplombe le centre-ville historique, la bibliothèque municipale de Halmstad a été pensée dans les moindres détails pour s'insérer harmonieusement dans son cadre. Le choix de matériaux simples, béton, verre et parquets en mélèze nordique, forme un espace lumineux et ouvert ; l'atrium, qui assure la liaison entre les trois niveaux, encercle un châtaigner sculptural, alors que la façade vitrée oblongue, de forme concave, inonde de lumière la bibliothèque, immergée en pleine nature. Le concept se prolonge vers l'extérieur où une forêt de colonnes surélève la bibliothèque au-dessus du niveau de la rue pour dominer l'étendue fluviale.

Situada en el parque del río Nissan, y con vistas al centro histórico de la ciudad, todos los elementos de la Biblioteca Municipal de Halmstad se han tenido en cuenta con respecto a su ubicación. Unos materiales sencillos (hormigón, cristal y revestimiento para suelos de alerce nórdico) conforman un espacio brillante y abierto; el atrio, que une los tres niveles, rodea un castaño escultural. La fachada acristalada grande y cóncava inunda la biblioteca de luz y la sume en plena naturaleza. Esta idea prosigue en el exterior, donde un bosque de columnas eleva la biblioteca sobre el nivel de la calle y sobre el agua.

Named after the Brothers Grimm, this library is comprised of two components of differing heights: the first blends in with the surrounding Berlin architecture, and the second, at 38 metres, asserts the library as a public landmark. Its stern exterior is interrupted by the contrasting rhythm of the windows – narrow for bookshelves, wider at workstations. Internally, an atrium with a glass roof is enveloped by five storeys of cherrywood terraces. The symmetry and the sparse use of materials create a peaceful atmosphere; the quiet sense of rhythm pervades.

Diese nach den Brüdern Grimm benannte Bibliothek setzt sich aus zwei Bauteilen unterschiedlicher Höhe zusammen, von denen das erste harmonisch mit der umliegenden Berliner Stadtlandschaft verschmilzt, während das zweite mit seinen 38 Metern Höhe für die gewünschte Sichtbarkeit dieses öffentlichen Wahrzeichens sorgt. Das strenge Exterieur der Bibliothek wird vom kontrastierenden Rhythmus der Fenster durchbrochen, deren Breite variiert und in der Nähe der Arbeitsplätze größer ausfällt als an den Bücherregalen. Im Gebäudeinneren umrahmen fünfgeschossige Kirschholzterrassen ein mit einem Glasdach überspanntes Atrium. Die Symmetrie und die sparsame Verwendung der Baustoffe tauchen die Einrichtung in ein von friedvollen Rhythmen gekennzeichnetes Ambiente.

Baptisée d'après le nom des frères Grimm, cette bibliothèque s'organise autour de deux blocs de hauteur différente : si le premier se fond dans l'architecture berlinoise attenante, le second, à 38 mètres de haut, impose l'édifice comme une véritable référence du génie civil. L'aspect austère de l'extérieur est rythmé par les lignes contrastées que forment les rangées de fenêtres, étroites pour les étagères et plus larges pour les postes de travail. L'enceinte intérieure du bâtiment avec sa toiture vitrée est encerclée par des terrasses en bois de cerisier sur cinq niveaux. La symétrie et l'emploi minimaliste de matériaux confère au lieu une atmosphère paisible tout entière empreinte du rythme régulier imprimé par les lignes architecturales.

Jacob and Wilhelm Grimm Centre

Humboldt University, Berlin, Germany
Max Dudler, 2009

Jacob and Wilhelm Grimm Centre, Humboldt University, Berlin, Germany

Esta biblioteca, que lleva el nombre de los hermanos Grimm, presenta dos componentes a distintas alturas: el primero armoniza con la arquitectura berlinesa circundante y el segundo, a 38 metros de altura, reafirma la biblioteca como punto de referencia público. Su severo exterior se ve interrumpido por el ritmo contrastado de las ventanas: estrechas para las estanterías de libros y más amplias para los puestos de trabajo. En el interior, cinco plantas de terrazas de madera de cerezo rodean un atrio con un techo acristalado. La simetría y el uso escaso de materiales crean un ambiente tranquilo en el que predomina el silencioso sentido del ritmo.

Occupying a central role in the intellectual life of Berlin since the end of the Second World War, the Free University is one of the city's most symbolic institutions. The new library for the Faculty of Philology occupies a site created by uniting six of the university's courtyards. Its four storeys are contained within a naturally ventilated, bubble-like enclosure, and an inner membrane of translucent glass fibre filters the daylight, creating the optimum atmosphere for concentration. The library has become an architectural landmark, already earning the nickname 'The Berlin Brain'.

Die Freie Universität Berlin nimmt seit dem Ende des Zweiten Weltkriegs im Berliner Geistesleben eine herausragende Stellung ein und zählt zu den symbolträchtigsten Institutionen der Stadt. Sechs Innenhöfe der Universität bilden den Standort der neuen Bibliothek der Philologischen Fakultät. Die vier Geschosse dieser Einrichtung werden von einer natürlich belüfteten, blasenartigen Hülle umschlossen. Eine Innenmembran aus durchsichtiger Glasfaser filtert das Tageslicht und sorgt so für eine konzentrationsförderliche Atmosphäre. Die Bibliothek wurde rasch zu einem baulichen Wahrzeichen samt eigenem Spitznamen, der mit „Berliner Hirn" nicht besser gewählt werden könnte.

Occupant une place de premier ordre dans la vie intellectuelle berlinoise depuis la fin de la Seconde guerre mondiale, l'Université libre est l'une des institutions les plus emblématiques de la ville. La nouvelle bibliothèque destinée à la Faculté de philologie se dresse sur un site qui relie six des cours de l'université. La bibliothèque se déploie sur quatre niveaux enveloppés dans une structure ovoïde ventilée de manière naturelle. La membrane intérieure en fibres de verre translucides laisse filtrer la lumière du jour pour créer une atmosphère idéalement propice à la concentration. La bibliothèque s'impose aujourd'hui comme une œuvre maîtresse de l'architecture berlinoise, déjà affublée du sobriquet de 'Cerveau de Berlin'.

La Universidad Libre ha desempeñado un papel fundamental en la vida intelectual de Berlín desde el final de la Segunda Guerra Mundial y representa una de las instituciones más simbólicas de la ciudad. La nueva biblioteca de la Facultad de Filología ocupa una sede que se creó al unir seis de los patios de la universidad. Sus cuatro plantas están contenidas en un envoltorio en forma de burbuja, que cuenta con ventilación natural. Una membrana interna de fibra de vidrio translúcida filtra la luz del día, lo que crea un ambiente óptimo para la concentración. La biblioteca se ha convertido en una referencia arquitectónica, que ya se ha ganado el apodo de «El cerebro de Berlín».

Philological Library

Free University of Berlin, Germany
Foster + Partners, 2005

Philological Library, Free University of Berlin, Germany

Strahov Monastery Library

Prague, Czech Republic
Giovanni Domenico Orsi, 1679
Jan Ignaz Palliardi, 1797

Strahov Premonstratensian Monastery was founded in 1149. Its library endured a number of disturbances over the following five hundred years, but after the Thirty Years' War, it was established in the new Theological Hall. In the late eighteenth century, the Philosophical Hall was added to accommodate the growing collection. The stacks of the Baroque Theological Hall are topped with gilded wooden cartouches. In the early classical Philosophical Hall (1797) hidden spiral staircases lead to a gallery which allows access to the higher volumes, and a closer look at the majestic fresco.

Strahov Monastery Library, Prague, Czech Republic

Le couvent de l'ordre des Prémontrés de Strahov a été fondé en 1149. La bibliothèque du couvent, malgré maints rebondissements depuis plus de cinq cents ans, a finalement été établie, après la Guerre de Trente ans, dans la nouvelle Salle théologique. Fin du dix-huitième siècle, la Salle philosophique fut ajoutée pour abriter la collection grandissante de la bibliothèque. Ses rayonnages sont notamment recouverts de cartouches en boiseries dorées. La Salle philosophique, de style classique précoce (1797), dissimule un escalier en spirale qui conduit à une galerie permettant d'accéder aux volumes entreposés en hauteur, et donnant sur les majestueuses fresques aux plafonds.

Das Prämonstratenser-Kloster Strahov wurde im Jahr 1149 gegründet und seine Bibliothek musste während der darauffolgenden fünf Jahrhunderte so manche Unbill ertragen, bevor sie nach Ende des Dreißigjährigen Krieges in den neuen Theologischen Saal verlegt wurde. Im ausgehenden 18. Jahrhundert wurde ihr der Philosophische Saal hinzugefügt, um der stetig wachsenden Sammlung Herr zu werden. Die Bücherregale des barocken Theologischen Saals laufen nach oben hin in vergoldete geschnitzte Holzkartuschen aus und im frühklassizistischen Philosophischen Saal (1797) erlauben verborgene Wendeltreppen die Verwendung höher gelagerter Bände sowie die genauere Betrachtung des majestätischen Freskos.

El monasterio premostratense de Strahov se fundó en 1149. Su biblioteca pasó por diversos avatares durante los siguientes quinientos años pero después de la Guerra de los Treinta Años, se trasladó a la nueva Sala Teológica. A finales del siglo XVIII, se añadió la Sala Filosófica para acoger la creciente colección. Las estanterías de la Sala Teológica Barroca están coronadas con cartelas de madera doradas. En la Sala Filosófica Clásica Temprana (1797), unas escaleras en espiral ocultas conducen a una galería que permite acceder a los volúmenes más altos y admirar de cerca el majestuoso fresco.

The Admont Benedictine Monastery, founded in 1074, has spent almost one thousand years collecting and preserving manuscripts and artefacts, and its library has become one of Austria's most important cultural properties. The architecture and decor of the late Baroque library were heavily influenced by ideas of the Enlightenment; according to the architect Hueber, 'As with the mind, light should also fill the room.' The ceiling frescoes, by eighty-year-old Bartolomeo Altomonte, are also inspired by the Enlightenment, and in contrast, sculptor Josef Stammel's carvings include depictions of Death, the Last Judgement, Heaven and Hell.

Admont Library

Admont, Austria
Josef Hueber, 1776

Seit nunmehr beinahe tausend Jahren werden im 1074 begründeten Benediktinerstift Admont Manuskripte und Artefakte gesammelt und aufbewahrt, was diese Bibliothek zu einem der bedeutendsten Kulturgüter Österreichs werden ließ. Bauweise und Dekor dieser spätbarocken Bibliothek wurden sehr stark von den Ideen der Aufklärung beeinflusst, was ihr Erbauer Hueber folgendermaßen in Worte fasste: „Wie den Verstand soll auch den Raum Licht erfüllen." Auch die vom achtzigjährigen Bartolomeo Altomonte stammenden Deckenfresken sind den Idealen der Aufklärung verpflichtet und stehen somit in starkem Kontrast zu den Arbeiten des Bildhauers Josef Stammel, der den Tod, das Jüngste Gericht sowie den Himmel und die Hölle in seinen Skulpturen abbildete.

L'Abbaye bénédictine d'Admont, fondée en 1074, a consacré presque mille ans à recueillir et à préserver des manuscrits et des reliques, raison pour laquelle sa bibliothèque est devenue l'un des patrimoines culturels les plus importants d'Autriche. L'architecture et les décorations de cette bibliothèque du baroque tardif ont été largement influencées par les idées des Lumières ; d'après les paroles de son architecte, Josef Hueber, 'de même que l'esprit, la salle doit être inondée de lumière'. Les fresques des plafonds, réalisées par Bartolomeo Altomonte alors âgé de quatre-vingt ans, ont également été inspirées par les Lumières, et offrent un contraste saisissant avec les sculptures de Josef Stammel qui dépeignent la Mort, le Jugement dernier, le Paradis et l'Enfer.

El monasterio benedictino de Admont, fundado en 1074, se ha dedicado durante casi mil años a recopilar y conservar manuscritos y artefactos, y su biblioteca se ha convertido así en una de las propiedades culturales más importantes de Austria. La arquitectura y la decoración de la biblioteca, de estilo barroco tardío, estaban muy influidas por las ideas de la Ilustración; según el arquitecto Hueber, «A la vez que la mente, la luz debe llenar también la habitación». Los frescos del techo, realizados por el artista de ochenta años Bartolomeo Altomonte, están inspirados igualmente en la Ilustración, y en contraste, las tallas del escultor Josef Stammel incluyen representaciones de la Muerte, el Último Juicio, el Cielo y el Infierno.

Melk Monastery Library

Melk, Austria

Jakob Prandtauer, 1736

Benedictine monks have lived and worked at this site since 1089, and in the twelfth century a school was added to the monastery. Due to its fame and academic stature, Melk managed to escape dissolution under Emperor Joseph II in the late eighteenth century, survived the brunt of the Napoleonic and World Wars, and now its school caters to almost 900 pupils of both sexes. The library comprises twelve rooms, and comes second only to the church in terms of importance, a fact reflected in its opulent decor and the ceiling frescoes by Paul Troger, symbolising Faith and Science.

Schon ab dem Jahr 1089 lebten und arbeiteten Benediktinermönche an diesem Ort, dessen Kloster im 12. Jahrhundert um eine Schule erweitert wurde. Dank seiner Berühmtheit sowie seiner akademischen Bedeutung entging Melk im ausgehenden 18. Jahrhundert der Auflösung durch Kaiser Joseph II., überdauerte die Wucht der Napoleonischen sowie beider Weltkriege und dient heute beinahe 900 Schülerinnen und Schülern als Hort des Wissens. Die Bibliothek erstreckt sich über zwölf Räume und gilt gleich nach der Stiftskirche selbst als bedeutendstes Gebäude der Klosteranlage, was sich in ihrem opulenten Dekor und den Deckenfresken von Paul Troger widerspiegelt, die Glaube und Wissenschaft symbolisieren.

L'abbaye est occupée par des moines bénédictins depuis 1089. Une école y fut annexée au douzième siècle. Grâce à sa renommée et à son statut académique, Melk échappa à la fermeture sous l'Empereur Joseph II à la fin du dix-huitième siècle, et survécu aux guerres napoléoniennes ainsi qu'aux guerres mondiales. Son école accueille aujourd'hui près de 900 élèves des deux sexes. Composée de douze salles, la bibliothèque talonne le monastère en termes d'importance, comme l'atteste ses décorations intérieures opulentes et la fresque de son plafond signée Paul Troger, allégorie de la Foi et de la Science.

Los monjes benedictinos llevan viviendo y trabajando en este lugar desde 1089 y, en el siglo XII, se añadió una escuela al monasterio. Debido a su fama y a su importancia académica, Melk logró salvarse de la disolución bajo el emperador José II a finales del siglo XVIII. Sobrevivió además a los desastres de las Guerras napoleónicas y mundiales, y ahora su escuela se ocupa de unos 900 alumnos de ambos sexos. La biblioteca consta de doce salas y solo es superada por la iglesia en términos de importancia, un hecho que se refleja en su opulenta decoración y en los frescos del techo de Paul Troger, que simbolizan la Fe y la Ciencia.

Austrian National Library

Vienna, Austria

Johann Bernhard Fischer von Erlach, 1726

The beginnings of this former court library go back to the second half of the fourteenth century. It is now the largest library in Austria, with more than 7 million objects, of which approximately 3 million are printed. Situated in the Hofburg Palace, and cathedral-like in its scale, the centrepiece is the Baroque State Hall, which is separated into wings representing War and Peace. These are crowned with lavish frescoes by Daniel Gran, and in the centre, beneath the cupola, a fresco combines allegorical and secular representations of the history and virtues of the library's bibliophile founders, the Habsburgs.

Der Ursprung dieser früheren Hofbibliothek liegt in der zweiten Hälfte des 14. Jahrhunderts. Mit über sieben Millionen Artikeln, darunter ungefähr drei Millionen gedruckten Werken, ist sie heute die größte Bibliothek Österreichs. Untergebracht ist diese, ihrer Größe nach bisweilen an eine Kathedrale erinnernde Bibliothek in der Wiener Hofburg. Das Herzstück der Anlage bildet der barocke Prunksaal, der in einen Kriegs- und einen Friedensflügel unterteilt ist. Gekrönt wird das Ganze durch aufwendige Fresken von Daniel Gran und in der Mitte unterhalb der Kuppel feiern allegorische und profane Darstellungen die Geschichte sowie die Tugenden jener bibliophilen Habsburger, die diese Bibliothek einst begründeten.

L'origine de cette ancienne bibliothèque de la Cour remonte à la seconde moitié du quatorzième siècle. Elle est aujourd'hui la plus grande bibliothèque d'Autriche, avec plus de 7 millions de pièces, dont près de 3 millions d'ouvrages imprimés. La bibliothèque a été construite dans le Palais Hofburg sur le modèle d'une cathédrale. Sa pièce maîtresse réside dans la salle d'apparat de style baroque, séparée en deux ailes représentant chacune la Guerre et la Paix, et décorées de fresques somptueuses signées Daniel Gran. En son centre, sous la coupole, on peut y admirer une fresque associant des représentations allégoriques et séculières de l'histoire et des vertus des fondateurs bibliophiles de l'édifice, les Habsbourg.

Los inicios de esta antigua biblioteca de la corte se remontan a la segunda mitad del siglo XIV. En la actualidad, es la mayor biblioteca de Austria, con más de siete millones de objetos, de los cuales tres millones aproximadamente están impresos. Situada en el Palacio de Hofburg y con un tamaño similar al de una catedral, su punto fuerte es el Salón de Estado barroco, dividido en dos alas que representan la Guerra y la Paz. Éstas están rematadas por espléndidos frescos de Daniel Gran, y en el centro, bajo la cúpula, un fresco combina representaciones alegóricas y seculares de la historia y las virtudes de los fundadores bibliófilos de la biblioteca, los Habsburgos.

Austrian National Library, Vienna, Austria

Austrian National Library, Vienna, Austria

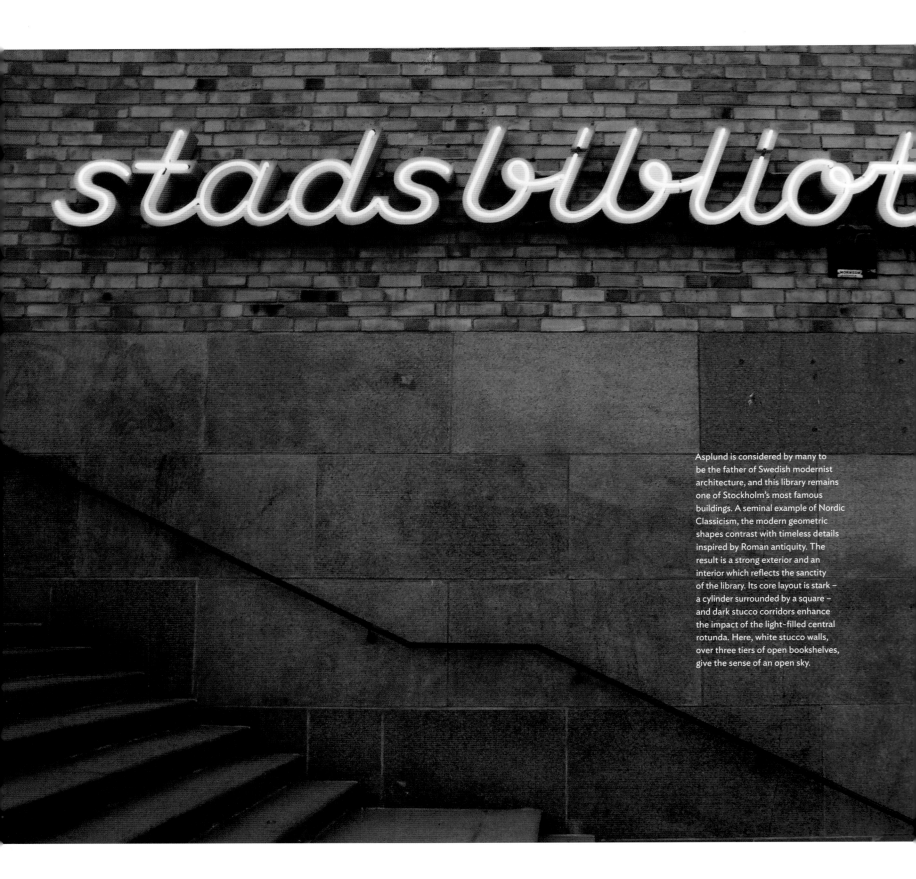

Asplund is considered by many to be the father of Swedish modernist architecture, and this library remains one of Stockholm's most famous buildings. A seminal example of Nordic Classicism, the modern geometric shapes contrast with timeless details inspired by Roman antiquity. The result is a strong exterior and an interior which reflects the sanctity of the library. Its core layout is stark – a cylinder surrounded by a square – and dark stucco corridors enhance the impact of the light-filled central rotunda. Here, white stucco walls, over three tiers of open bookshelves, give the sense of an open sky.

Stockholm Public Library

Stockholm, Sweden
Erik Gunnar Asplund, 1928

Asplund est considéré par beaucoup comme le père de l'architecture moderniste suédoise. Cette bibliothèque demeure l'un des bâtiments les plus emblématiques de Stockholm. Œuvre fondatrice du Classicisme nordique, les formes géométriques modernes de la bibliothèque contrastent avec les détails intemporels inspirés de l'antiquité romaine. Derrière un extérieur imposant, l'intérieur est à l'image du caractère sacré que revêt la bibliothèque. Sa disposition centrale frappe par son austérité, un cylindre entouré d'un carré, alors que les couloirs en stuc sombre contribuent à renforcer l'atmosphère lumineuse que projette la rotonde centrale, dont les murs en stuc blanc parcourus de trois niveaux d'étagères accessibles donnent l'impression d'être à ciel ouvert.

Asplund está considerado por muchos como el padre de la arquitectura modernista sueca y esta biblioteca sigue siendo uno de los edificios más famosos de Estocolmo. Ejemplo fundamental de clasicismo nórdico, las modernas formas geométricas contrastan con los detalles intemporales inspirados en la antigüedad romana. El resultado es un exterior que deja huella y un interior que refleja el carácter sagrado de la biblioteca. Su trazado principal es escueto: un cilindro rodeado por un cuadrado. Los pasillos de estuco oscuro realzan el impacto de la luminosa rotonda central. Aquí, las paredes de estuco claro, sobre tres niveles de estanterías de libros despejadas, dan la impresión de estar a cielo abierto.

Erik Gunnar Asplund gilt vielen als Vater der modernen schwedischen Architektur und seine stadsbibliotek ist und bleibt eines der berühmtesten Bauwerke Stockholms. Die modernen geometrischen Formen dieses wegweisenden Beispiels des Nordischen Klassizismus stehen in scharfem Kontrast zu den ebenfalls verwendeten zeitlosen und aus der römischen Antike entlehnten Details. Das Ergebnis ist ein robustes Äußeres einerseits und ein die Unantastbarkeit der Bibliothek widerspiegelndes Inneres andererseits. Der schlichte Grundriss in Form eines von einem Quadrat umrahmten Zylinders sowie die dunklen, stuckverzierten Korridore verstärken die Wirkung der lichtdurchfluteten zentralen Rotunde, wo weiße Stuckwände über den in drei Ebenen angeordneten offenen Bücherregalen an einen grenzenlosen Himmel erinnern.

Photography Credits

Library of Alexandria
p. 10 Scanpix/Camera Press
p. 12 Camera Press
p. 13 Paul Doyle/Getty Images
p. 14/5 Hisham Ibrahim/
Getty Images

Russian State Library
p. 16 Jonathan Smith/
Getty Images
p. 17 Jochen Helle/
Artur Images

King Fahd National Library
p. 18 Christian Richters
p. 19 Christian Richters
p. 20 Christian Richters
p. 21 Christian Richters

LiYuan Library
p. 22 Li Xiaodong Atelier
p. 23 Li Xiaodong Atelier
p. 24/5 Li Xiaodong Atelier
p. 26 Li Xiaodong Atelier
p. 27 Li Xiaodong Atelier

Hachioji Library
p. 28/9 Edmund Sumner/View/
Artur Images
p. 30 Edmund Sumner/View/
Artur Images
p. 31 Edmund Sumner/View/
Artur Images

State Library of Victoria
p. 32 Richard Nebesky/
Getty Images
p. 33 Christopher Groenhout/
Getty Images
p. 34/5 EschCollection/
Getty Images

Seattle Central Library
p. 36 Frank Elschner/
Artur Images
p. 37 Frank Elschner/
Artur Images
p. 38/9 Frank Elschner/
Artur Images

José Vasconcelos Library
p. 40 Ed Reeve/View/
Artur Images
p. 41 Ed Reeve/View/
Artur Images
p. 42/3 Ed Reeve/View/
Artur Images

Library of Congress
p. 44 Oleg Albinsky/
Getty Images
p. 45 Camera Press
p. 46/7 Laif/Camera Press

George Peabody Library
p. 48 Panoramic Images/
Getty Images
p. 49 Greg Pease/Getty Images
p. 50/1 Michael Saft

Biblioteca España
p. 52 Biblioteca España
p. 53 John Coletti/Getty Images
p. 54 Biblioteca España
p. 55 Biblioteca España
p. 56/7 Miple Kim

New York Public Library
p. 58/9 Julia Cawley/
Artur Images
p. 60 Reinhard Görner/
Artur Images
p. 61 Phil Evans
p. 62/3 Reinhard Görner/
Artur Images

Royal Portuguese Reading Room
p. 64 Ruy Barbosa Pinto/
Getty Images
p. 65 Laif/Camera Press
p. 66/7 Edu Mendes

TEA Tenerife Arts Space
p. 68 Hufton + Crow/View/
Artur Images
p. 69 Inigo Bujedo Aguirre/
View/Artur Images
p. 70 Hufton + Crow/View/
Artur Images
p. 71 Hufton + Crow/View/
Artur Images

Joanina Library
p. 72 Paul Mazumdar
p. 73 Gamma-Rapho

National Library of Ireland
p. 74 IIC/Axiom/Getty Images
p. 75 National Library of Ireland
p. 76/7 Semmick Photo/
Shutterstock.com

Trinity College Library
p. 78 Ingram Publishing/
Getty Images
p. 79 Stefano Scata/
Getty Images
p. 80 Doug McKinlay/
Getty Images
p. 81 Mark Colliton

Glasgow School of Art Library
p. 82 Laif/Camera Press
p. 83 Chris Close/Getty Images

Library of El Escorial
p. 84/5 Photo by cuellar/
Getty Images
p. 86 Laif/Camera Press
p. 87 Arturo R. Montesinos

Sir Duncan Rice Library
p. 88 Adam Mørk
p. 89 Adam Mørk
p. 90 Adam Mørk
p. 91 Adam Mørk
p. 92/3 Adam Mørk

Library of Birmingham
p. 94 Christian Richters
p. 95 Christian Richters

British Library
p. 96 Peter Barritt/Getty Images
p. 97 British Library/Robana/
Getty Images

Peckham Library and Media Centre
p. 98/9 Richard Glover/View/
Artur Images
p. 100 Richard Glover/View/
Artur Images
p. 101 James Morris/View/
Artur Images
p. 102/3 James Morris/View/
Artur Images

Sainte-Geneviève Library
p. 104 Laif/Camera Press
p. 105 Yvonne Martejevs
p. 106/7 Paula Soler-Moya

Dipòsit de les Aigües Library
p. 108 Simón García
p. 109 Simón García
p. 110/1 Simón García
p. 111 Simón García

Book Mountain
p. 112 Jeroen Musch
p. 113 Jeroen Musch
p. 114/5 Jeroen Musch

TU Delft Library
p. 116/7 M. Sleeuwits/TU Delft
p. 118 TU Delft
p. 119 View Pictures/
Getty Images
p. 120/1 J. van der Heul/TU Delft

John a Lasco Library
p. 122 Tomas Riehle/
Artur Images
p. 123 Tomas Riehle/
Artur Images
p. 124/5 Tomas Riehle/
Artur Images

Vennesla Library and Culture House
p. 126/7 Hufton + Crow/View/
Artur Images
p. 128 Hufton + Crow/View/
Artur Images
p. 129 Hufton + Crow/View/
Artur Images

Library of the Faculty of Law, University of Zurich
p. 130 Monika Nikolic/
Artur Images
p. 131 Monika Nikolic/
Artur Images
p. 132 Monika Nikolic/
Artur Images
p. 133 Monika Nikolic/
Artur Images

Stuttgart City Library
p. 134 Axel Hausberg/
Artur Images
p. 135 Axel Hausberg/
Artur Images
p. 136/7 Axel Hausberg/
Artur Images

Abbey Library of St Gall
p. 138 Stiftsbibliothek St Gallen
p. 139 Stiftsbibliothek St Gallen
p. 140/1 Stiftsbibliothek St Gallen

Laurentian Library
p. 142 Firenze, Biblioteca
Medicea Laurenziana,
Settore Monumentale …
Su concessione del
Ministero per i Beni e
le Attività Culturali.
E'vietata ogni ulteriore
riproduzione con
qualsiasi mezzo.
p. 143 Firenze, Biblioteca
Medicea Laurenziana,
Settore Monumentale …
Su concessione del
Ministero per i Beni e
le Attività Culturali.
E'vietata ogni ulteriore
riproduzione con
qualsiasi mezzo.

Duchess Anna Amalia Library
p. 144/5 Gerhard Hagen/
Artur Images
p. 146 Werner Huthmacher/
Artur Images
p. 147 Werner Huthmacher/
Artur Images

Luckenwalde Library
p. 148 Thomas Lewandovski
p. 149 Thomas Lewandovski

The Black Diamond, Royal Library of Denmark
p. 150/1 Ralph Richter
p. 152 Adam Mørk
p. 153 Adam Mørk
p. 154 Jørgen True
p. 155 Jørgen True

Halmstad City Library
p. 156/7 Adam Mørk
p. 158 Adam Mørk
p. 159 Adam Mørk

Jacob and Wilhelm Grimm Centre
p. 160/1 Thomas Lewandovski
p. 161 Thomas Lewandovski
p. 162/3 Thomas Lewandovski

Philological Library
p. 164 Benjamin Antony Monn/
Artur Images
p. 165 Reinhard Görner/
Artur Images
p. 166/7 Reinhard Görner/
Artur Images

Strahov Monastery Library
p. 168 Gamma-Rapho
p. 169 Gamma-Rapho
p. 170/1 Bango/Shutterstock.com

Admont Library
p. 172 Lasting Images/
Getty Images
p. 173 Lasting Images/
Getty Images
p. 174/5 Imagno/
Getty Images

Melk Monastery Library
p. 176 Danita Delimont/
Getty Images
p. 177 Laif/Camera Press
p. 178 Danita Delimont/
Getty Images
p. 179 Danita Delimont/
Getty Images

Austrian National Library
p. 180/1 Sylvain Sonnet/
Getty Images
p. 182 Laif/Camera Press
p. 183 Laif/Camera Press
p. 184/5 Andy Christiani/
Getty Images

Stockholm Public Library
p. 186/7 Fredrik Andersson
p. 187 Olle Norberg
p. 188 Klaus Frahm/Artur Images